The Josephy Center is excited to bring you our first ever Livestock Art Show! We've invited local farmer and rancher artists to submit work to our call for farm and ranch animals and any scenes or depictions of farm and ranch life.

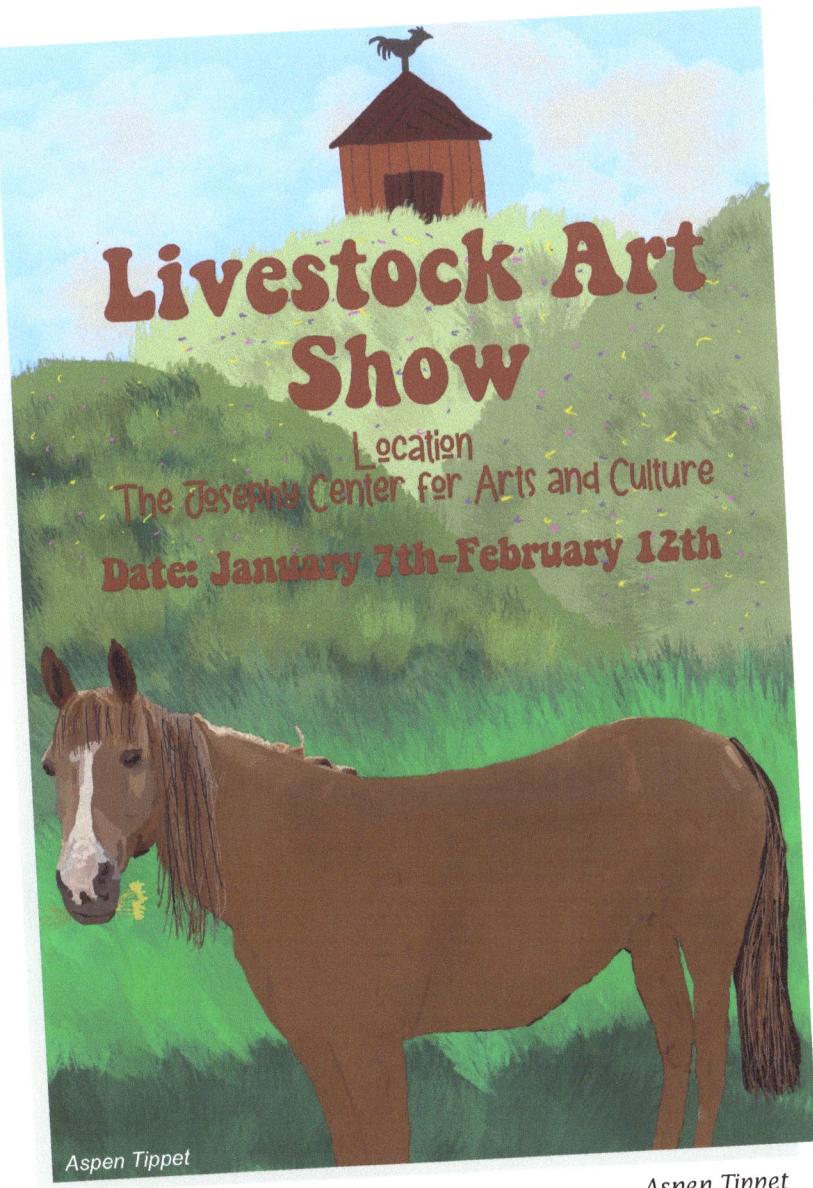

Poster Contest Winner

Aspen Tippet

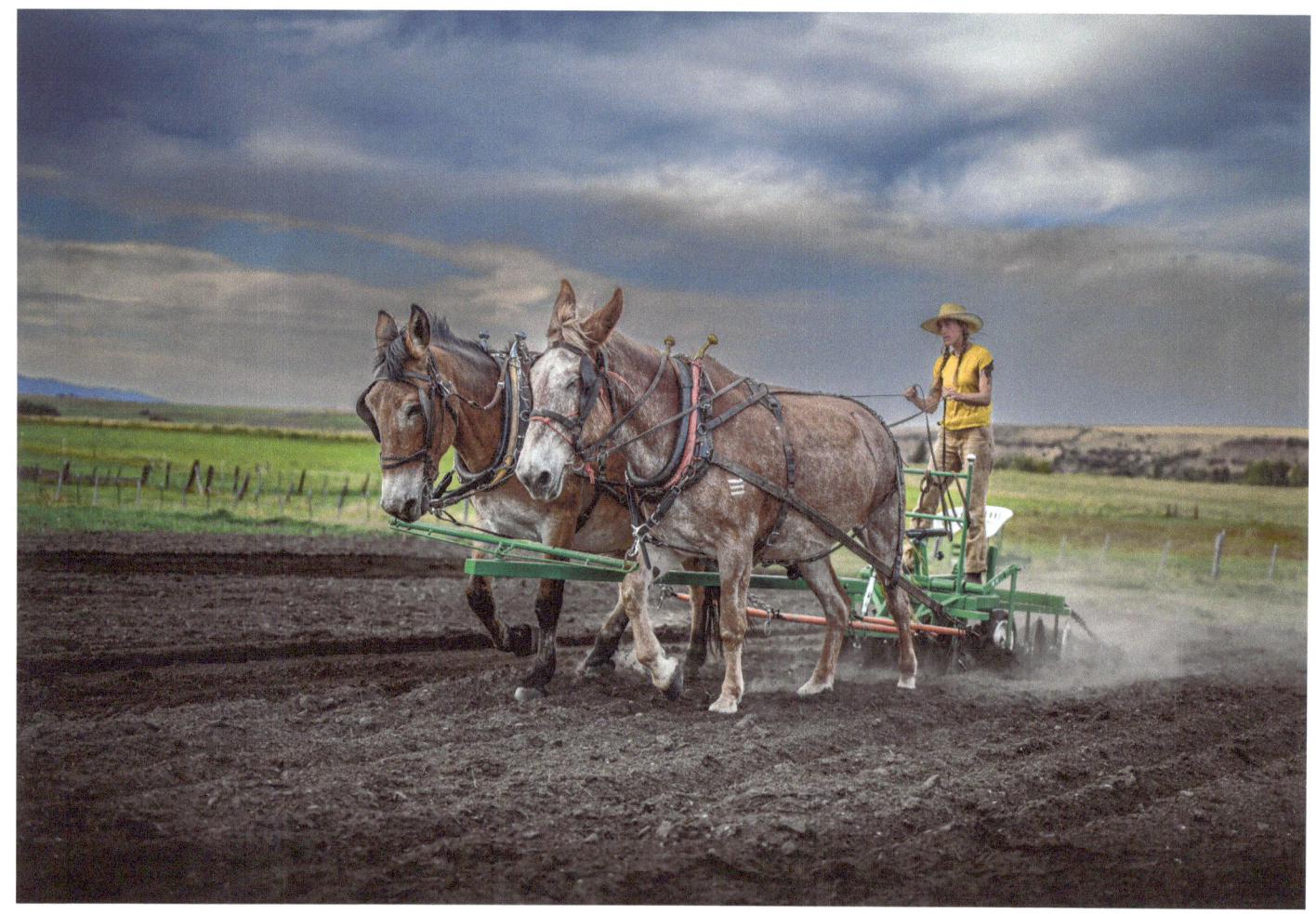

Racing The Rain

Paul Freidel

I am Paul Freidel, a photographer deeply rooted in the breathtaking landscapes of Wallowa County, Oregon. My lens is attuned to the intrinsic beauty of the Wallowa Valley, where the play of natural light, the vibrant energy of mountains, people, and animals, and the rugged allure of farm, ranch, and rodeo events come together in a harmonious dance. My wife and I live on a ranch in Lostine where we raise sheep, graze cows, and watch the bees make honey.

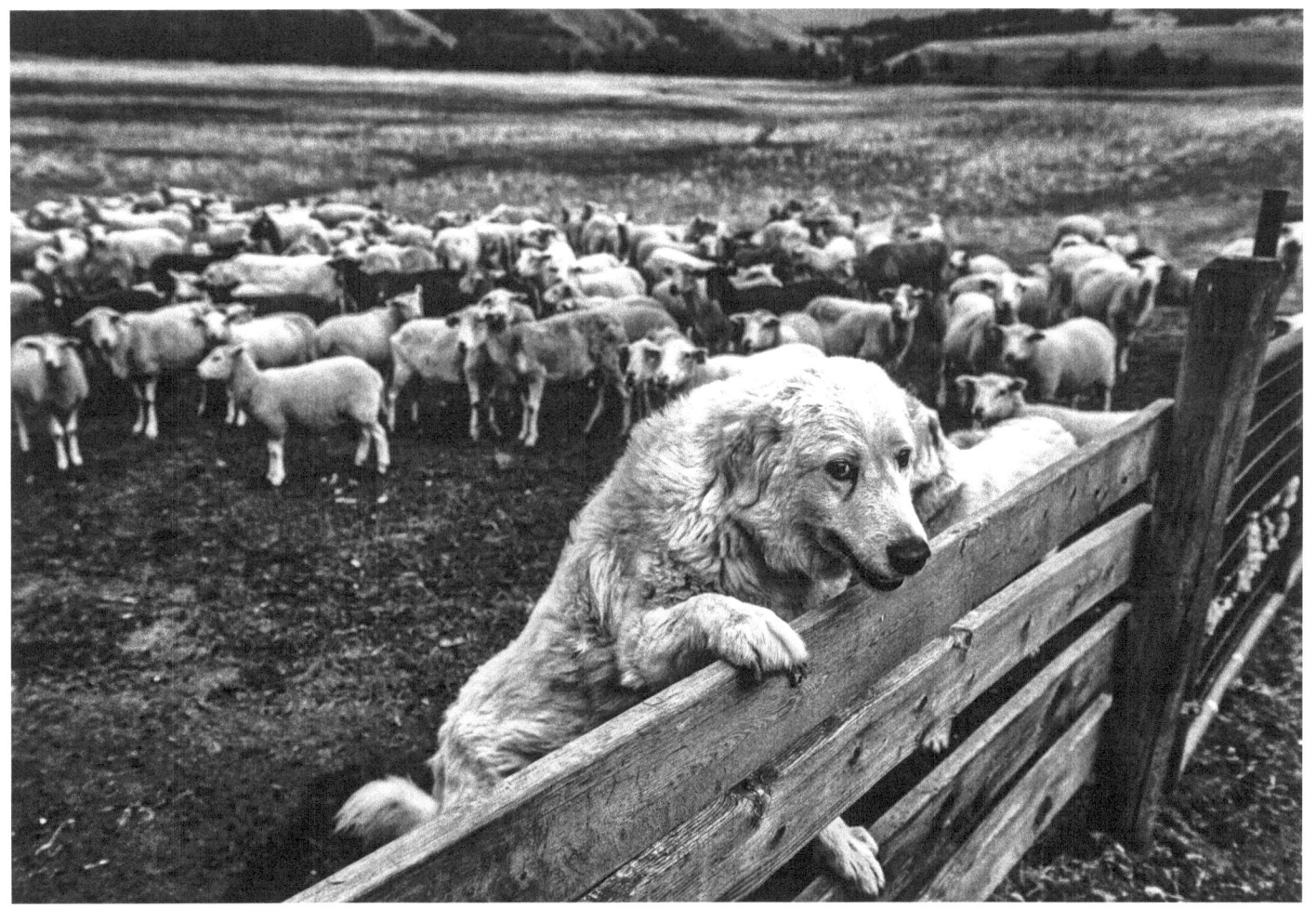

Zoey   *Paul Freidel*

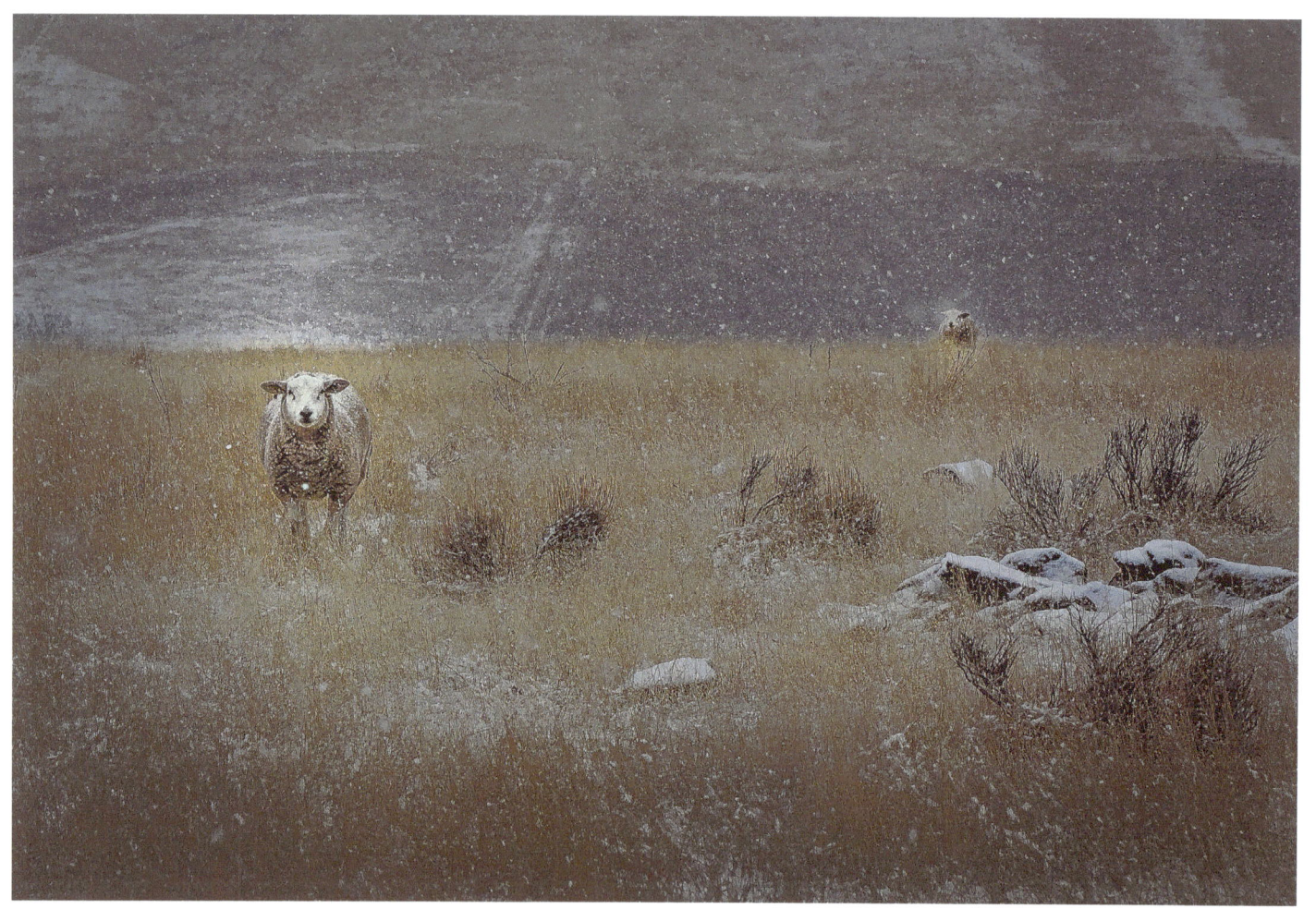

First Snow

Paul Freidel

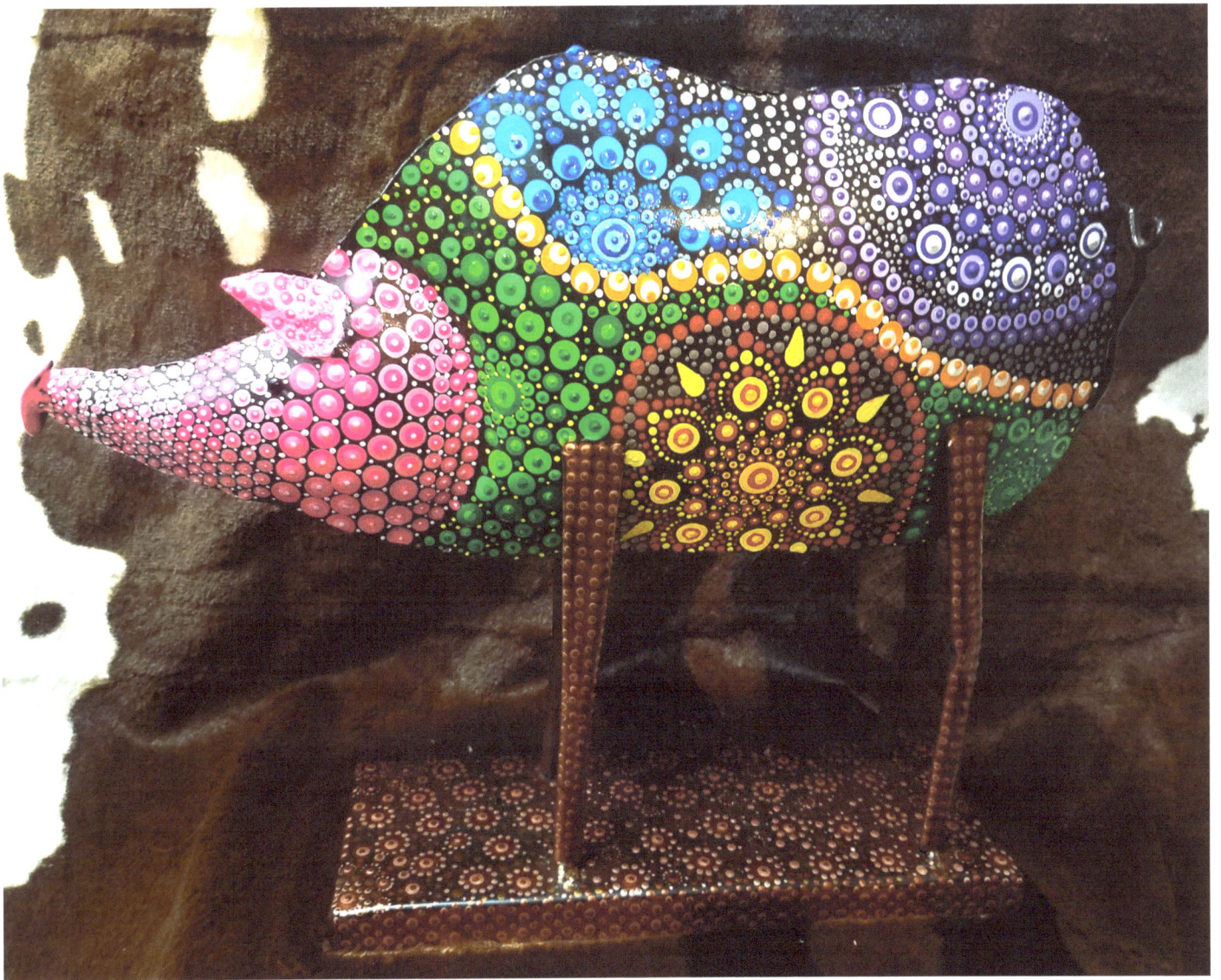

County Hog Turns City Girl   *Sondra Ross*

Local crafter, turned Dot Artist. I was raised on a cattle ranch in Central Oregon.
That lifestyle will always be the way I live.

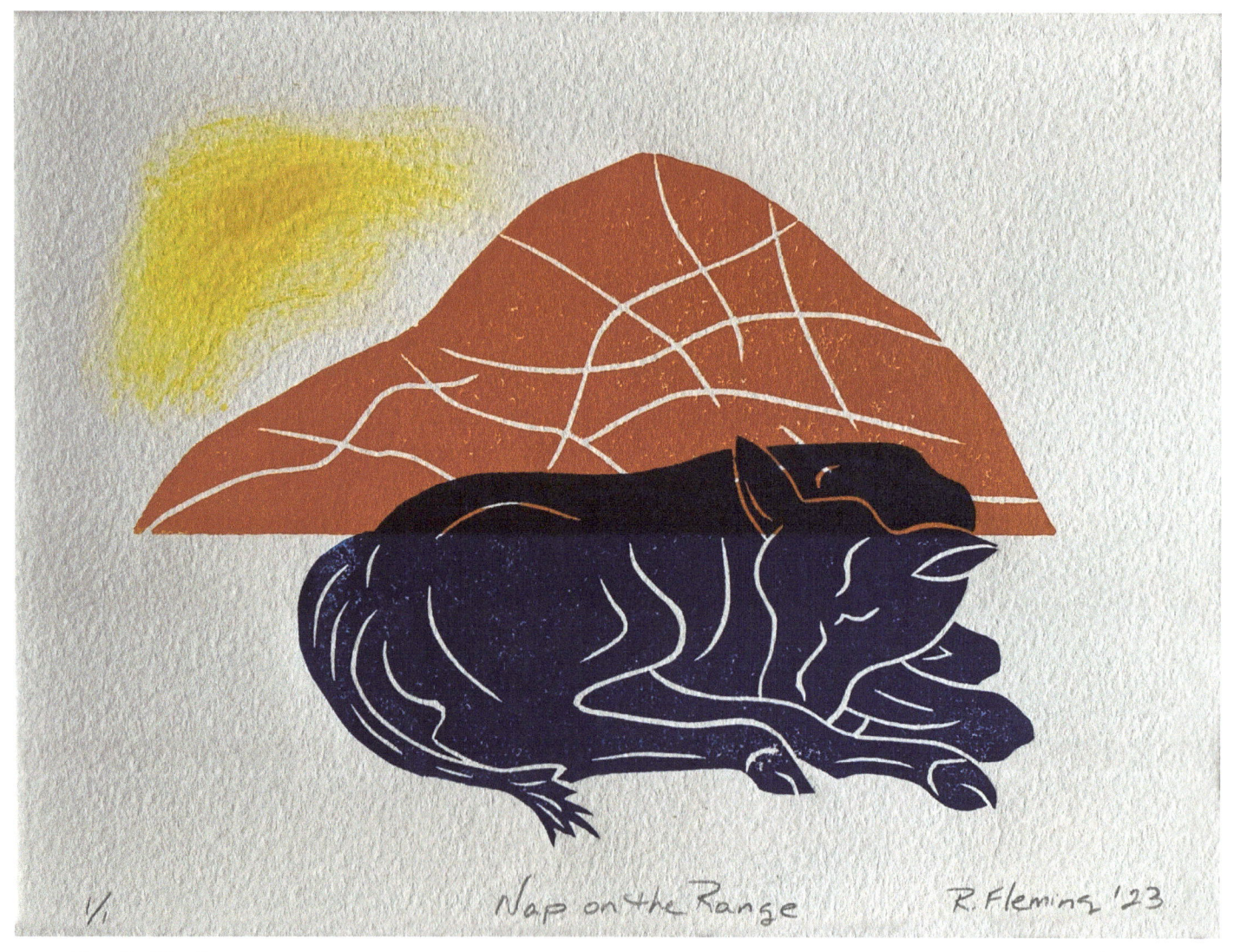

Nap On The Range   *Rene Fleming*

During my time as a veterinarian I was privileged to work with local ranchers. What I found was their close bond to their animals as well as a love for the land in which they lived and worked.

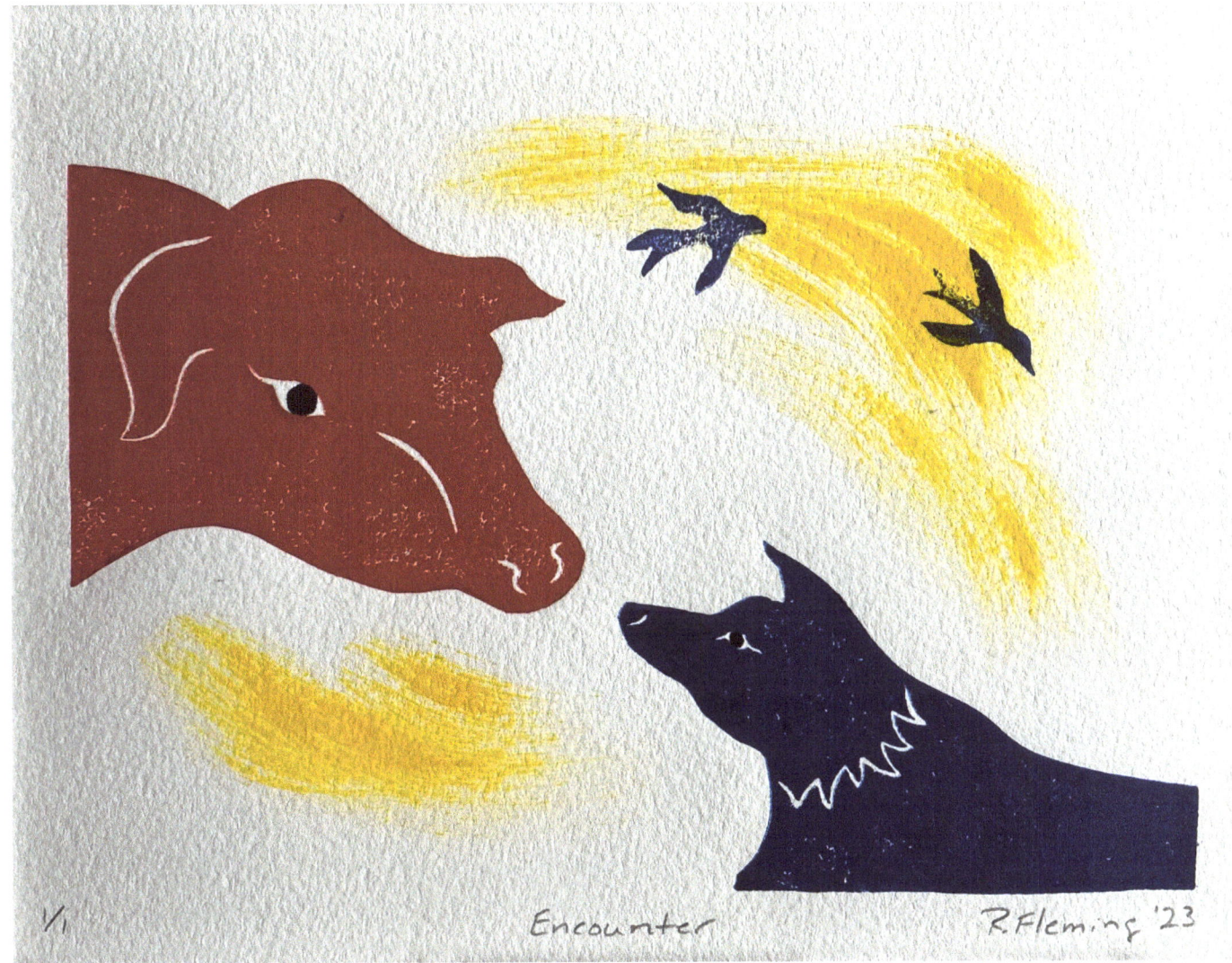

Encounter   *Rene Fleming*

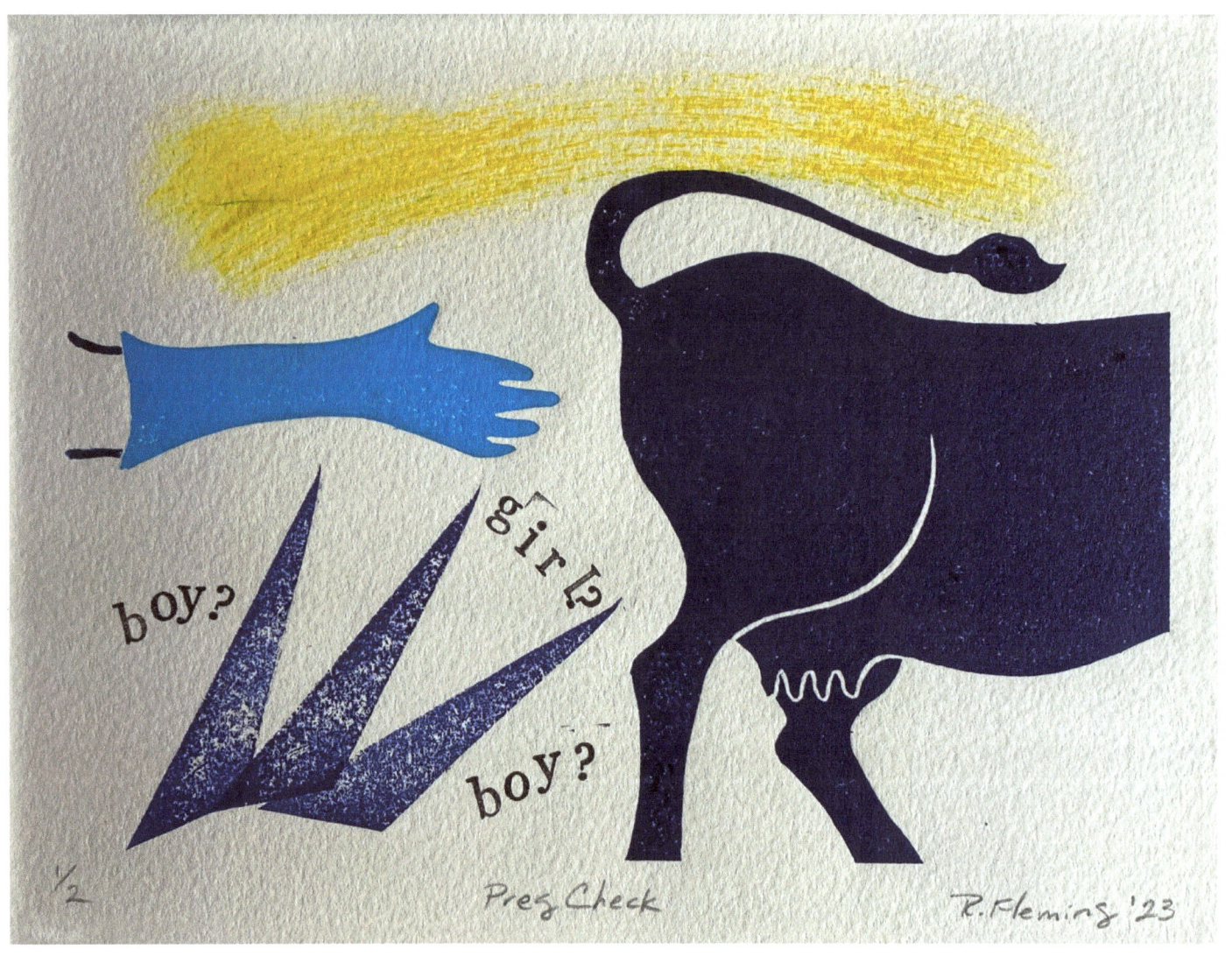

Preg Check   Rene Fleming

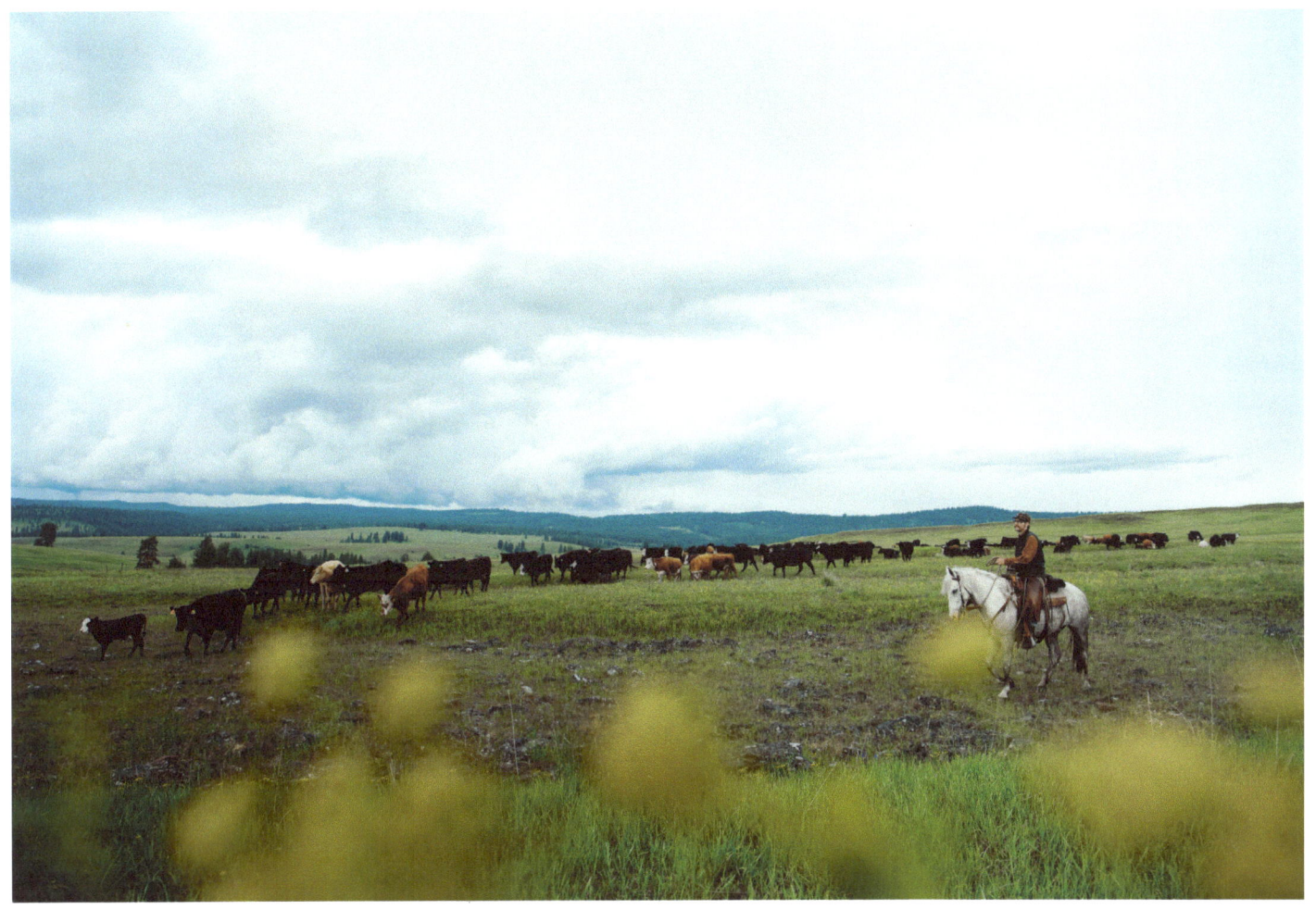

Spring Cattle   *Talia Filipek*

Talia Filipek lives in Joseph, Oregon and loves taking photos of wild babes and wild flowers.

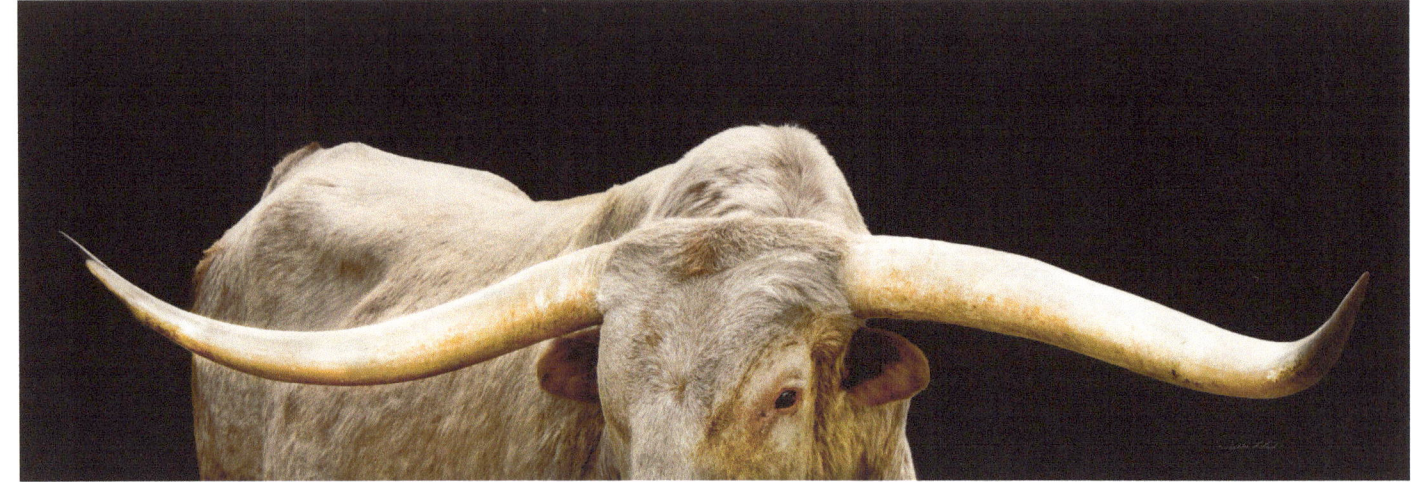

Duane The Longhorn   *Debbie Lind*

D. Lind Photo artisan is a distinguished and internationally recognized photographer with an unyielding passion for the art of photography. Over her 45 years of capturing life using her camera, her journey in the world of imagery has been nothing short of extraordinary. Debbie's remarkable talent has earned her numerous accolades, including prestigious Best of Show awards and Honorable Mentions, that have taken her work to Barcelona, Spain and shown at the FOTONOSTRUM GALLERY that span her illustrious career.

Specializing in the captivating realms of fractal and macro photography, Debbie's lens captures the hidden beauty in the world around us. Her discerning eye is drawn to a diverse range of subjects, including awe-inspiring landscapes, delicate flowers, extra ordinary sunsets, animals in all shapes and sizes and the compelling essence of individuals, and beyond. Her diverse portfolio showcases a deep connection with the multifaceted tapestry of life. Discovering her photography over 45 years tells her that art is not just about aesthetics, it's an artwork of rejuvenation offering you the calming embrace you crave coming home after a taxing day. Art whether you view it or create it, art nourishes positive feelings.

Debbie's photography is a testament to her dedication and innate talent, all cultivated through self-taught expertise and a deep-seated inspiration from her father, a photographer who meticulously processed black and white film in a bygone era. Furthering her artistic lineage, Debbie has drawn inspiration from the renowned Oregon Photographer Ray Atkeson, celebrated for his enchanting landscapes of the Pacific Northwest.

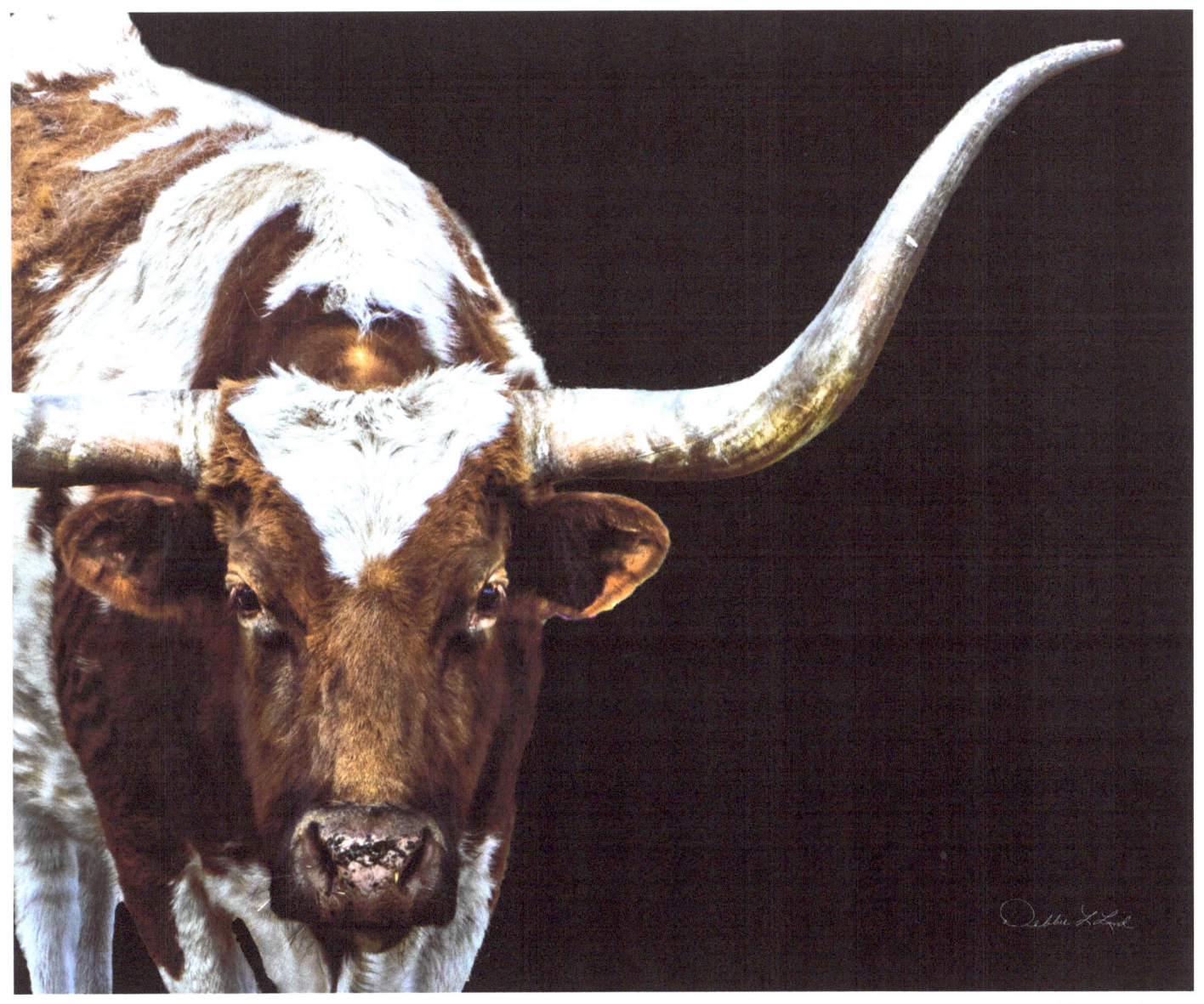

Gypsy   Debbie Lind

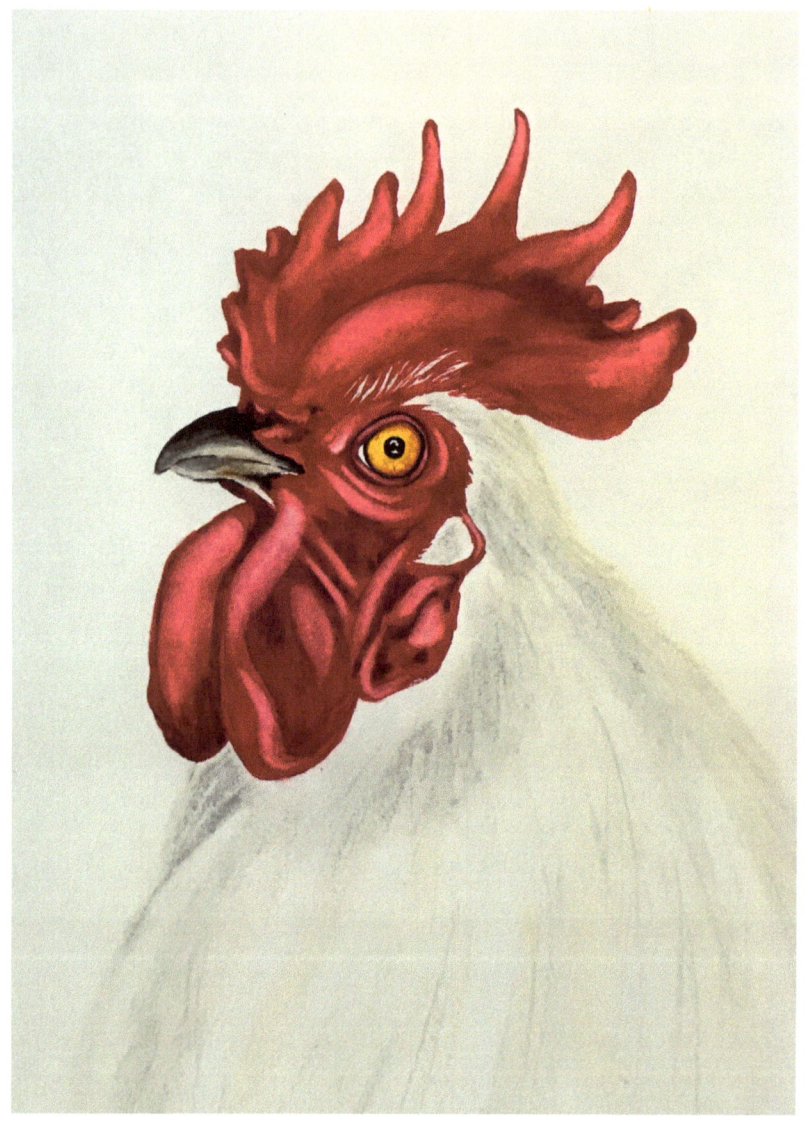

I may look calm ... but in my head   AMO
I've pecked you three times

AMO, an anonymous multimedia artist, draws inspiration from nature's fine details, crafting works that explore the delicate nuances often overlooked in the rush of daily life. Each piece challenges the artist's limits and beckons viewers to marvel in the beauty. Art is therapy. In a world where anonymity becomes a deliberate choice, AMO's legacy lies not in personal acclaim but in the collective wonder inspired by the intricacies of the natural world, beautifully realized through the artist's hands.

Memories of Fall Roundup

Lunch rolled up in a gunny sack, tied to the back of the saddle.

A peanut butter and jelly sandwich, an apple to share with her horse.

The meadow, inviting as it always was.

She slides from the saddle stretching the muscles already sore from the long
mornings ride.

Sitting on a log her dad nods toward the horses now grazing on the grass

still plentiful even after the cattle had been there all summer.

"You better watch him; he's going to leave you walking."

She rose and spoke softly to the small gelding, offering him the core of the apple.

The bond they shared stopped him from leaving her.

She would ride home today.

Nicola '23

Memories of Fall Roundup   *Nicola Norman*

Nicola was raised on a ranch in the north end of Wallowa county where she spent her days gardening, riding her horse and enjoying her dog and the farm cats. Her passions are her family, her dog and connecting with nature.

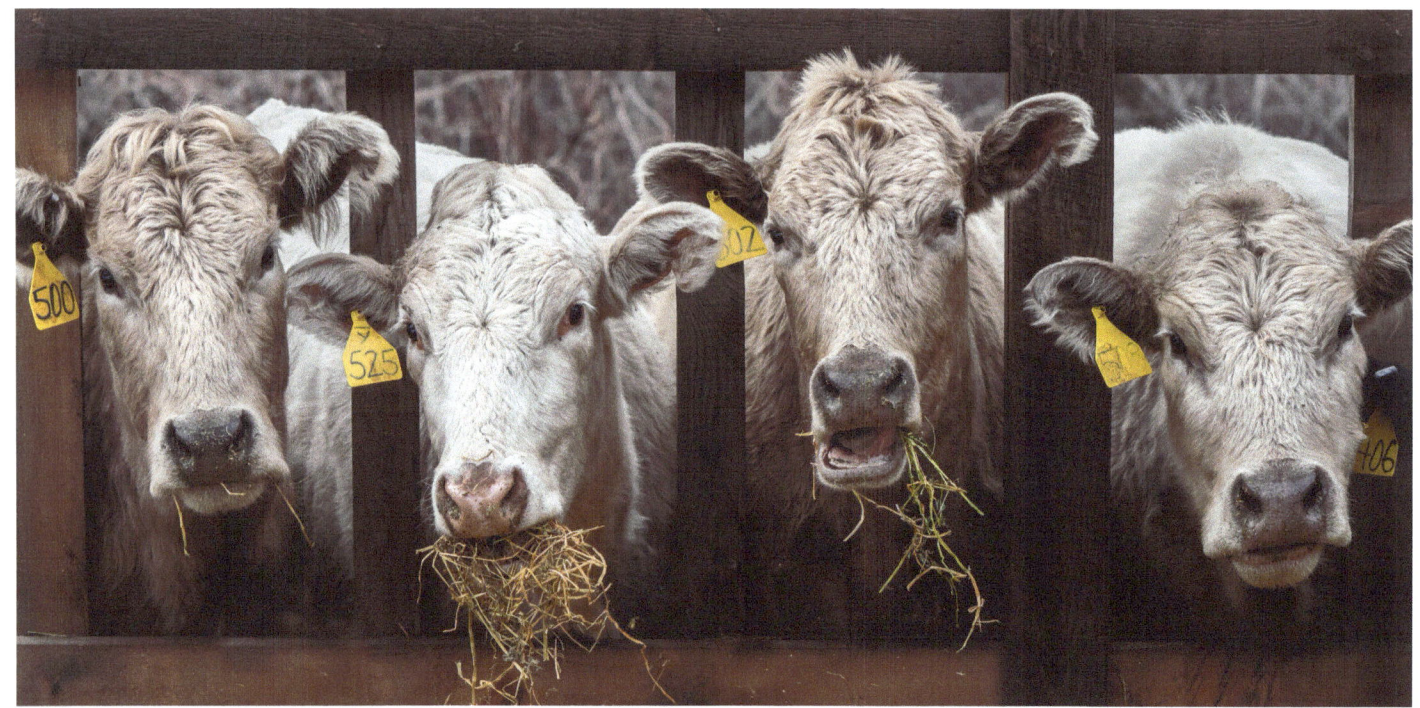

#500 #525 #502 #508   *Sven Geirmaert*

Sven is a passionate amateur nature photographer, print maker, and frame builder. He grew up in the lowlands of Belgium and quickly learned he needed to be closer to mountains. Come his late teens he had no idea what to do with his life and started traveling around the world, almost always carrying a camera with him. Finally realizing his need to work with people he decided to become a Social Worker. During an internship in Cambodia he met his now wife and moved to Portland in 2014 where he served the homeless. The search for a place to settle was on and after exploring much of the PNW the natural beauty and energy of Joseph lured them in. They moved in 2021 and are now expecting their first child. He happily works as a case manager for the Wallowa Valley Center for Wellness and loves exploring the county with his camera. For the longest time he only shared his work with a select few.
The coziness and welcoming nature of the Josephy Center gave him the courage to start showing his work to a larger public, something he's very grateful for.

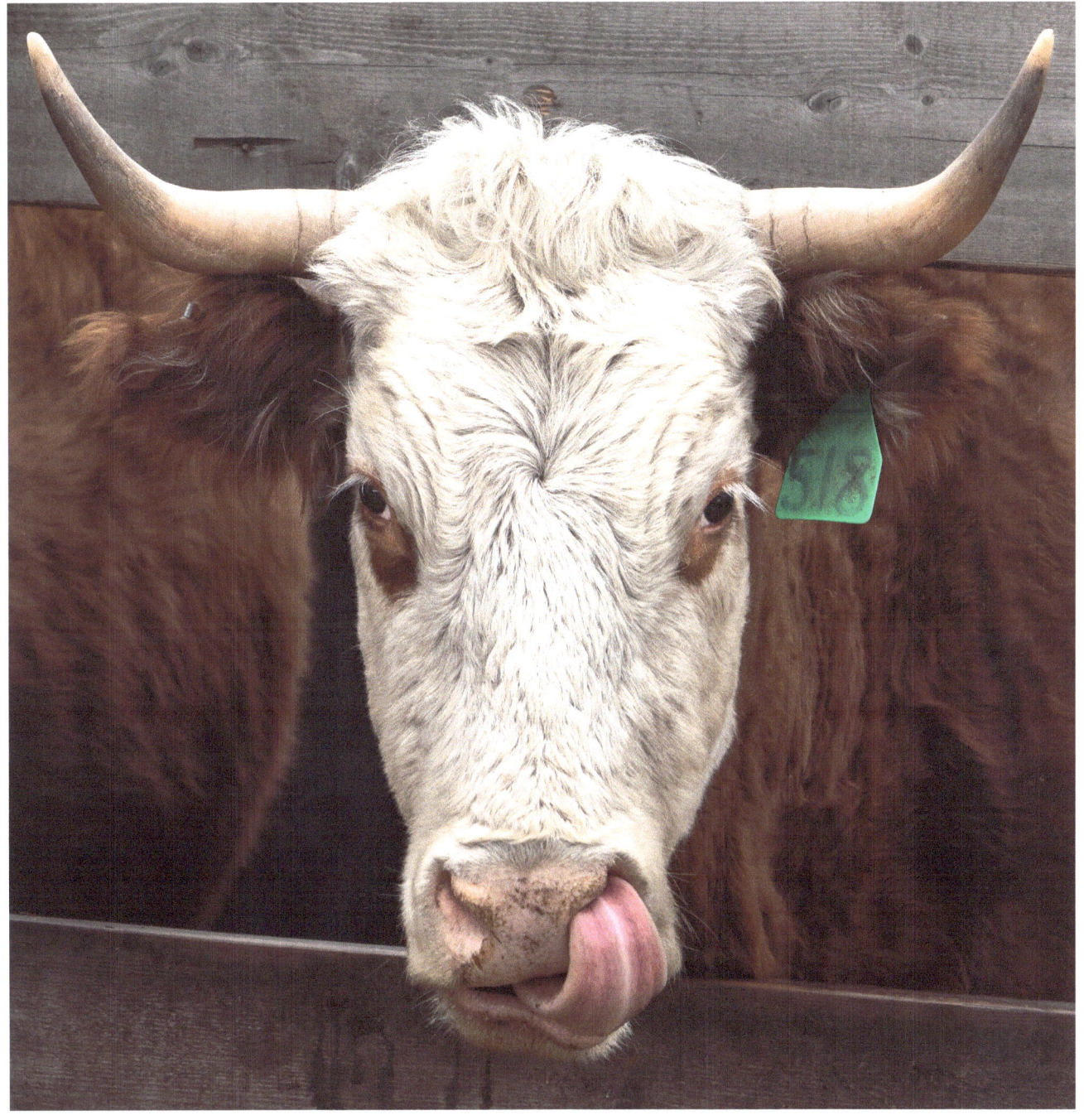

Seduce Me   *Sven Geirmaert*

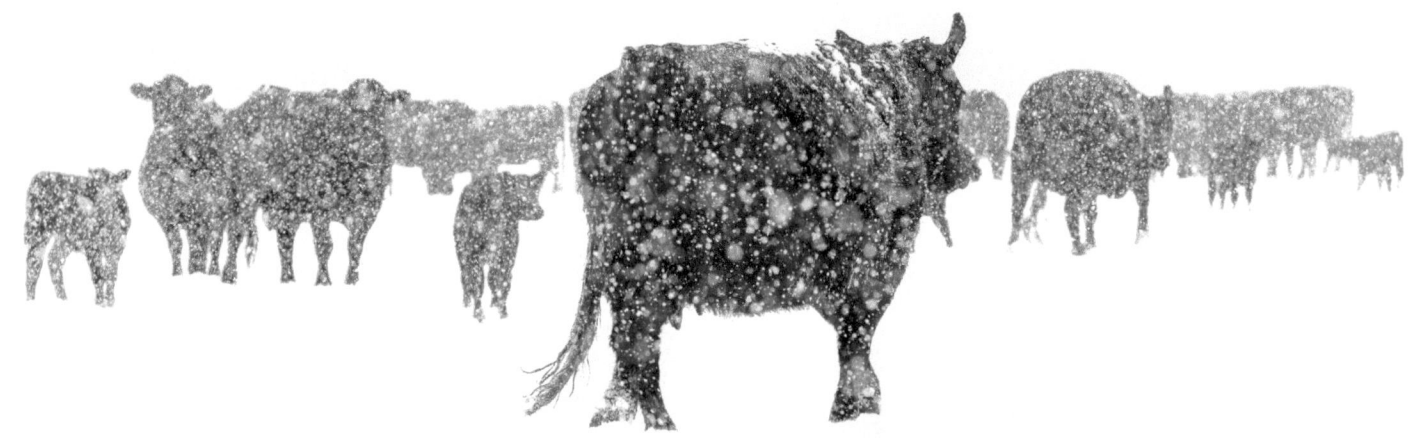

Back To The Snow   *Sven Geirmaert*

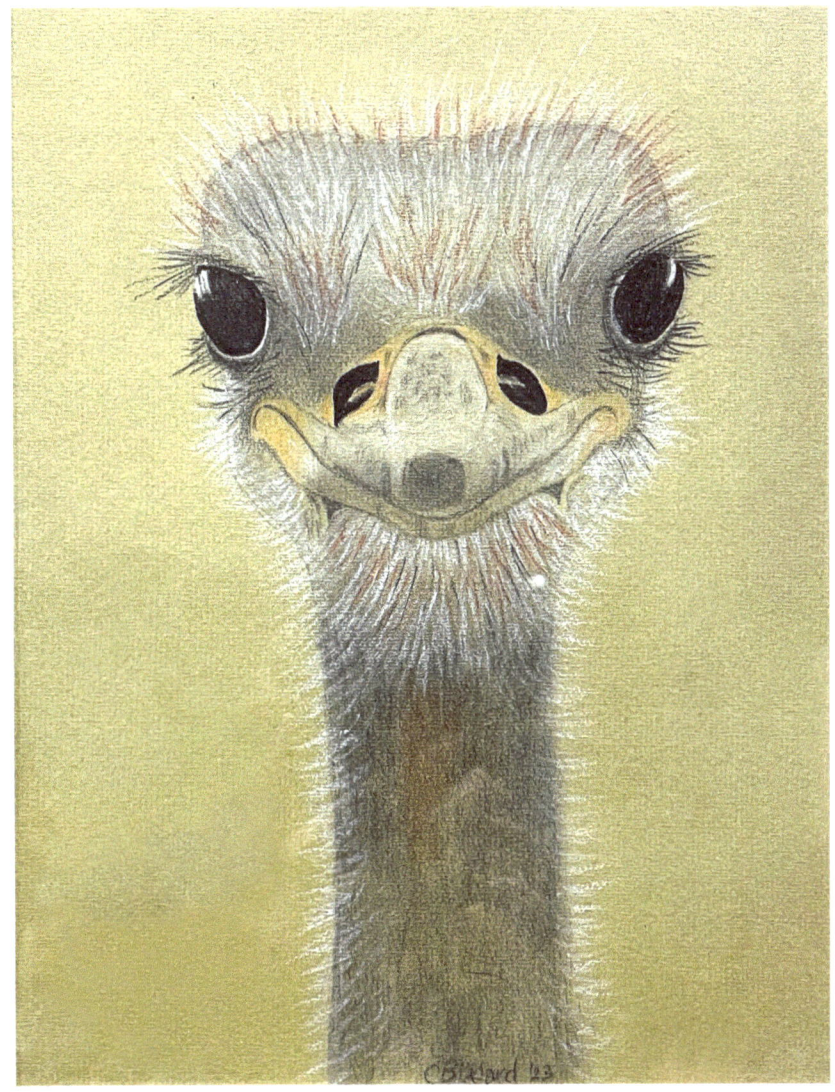

Bird's Eye View   *Eloise Stolsig*

Born and raised in Wallowa County. Grew up on Lightning Creek Ranch. Moved back to the county three years ago. My husband Frank and I spend winters in Arizona. I have been drawing and painting off and on my whole life. Hoping to do more now that I am retired.

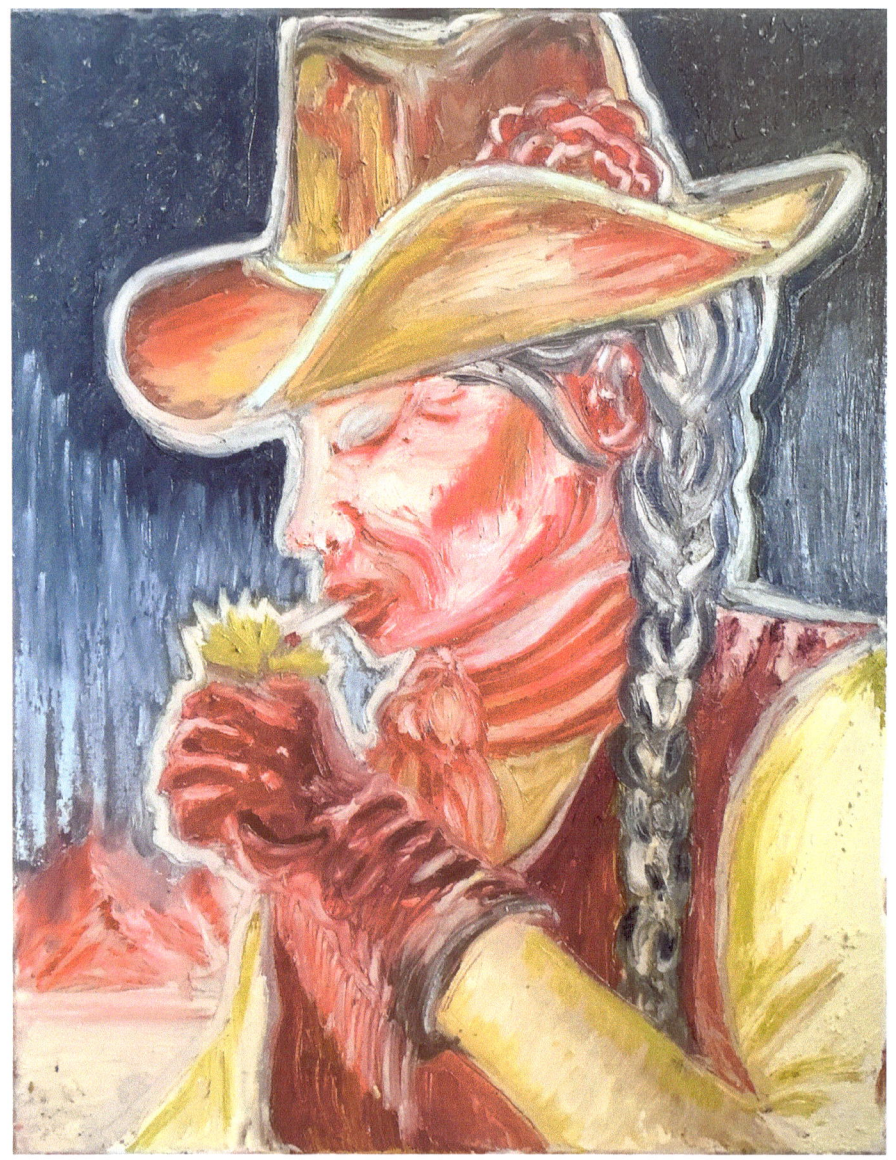

Workin' Woman Blues   *Autumn Roseberry*

I moved to Wallowa County in 2021 from rural SE Alaska. My husband and I own the Lostine Tavern and that takes up the majority of my time these days, but whenever I can sneak away to create art in multiple forms. Lately I have been working with oil pigment sticks, which allows me to apply oil paint directly to canvas with no brush, pallet knife or other tools to get in the way, which is how this piece was created.

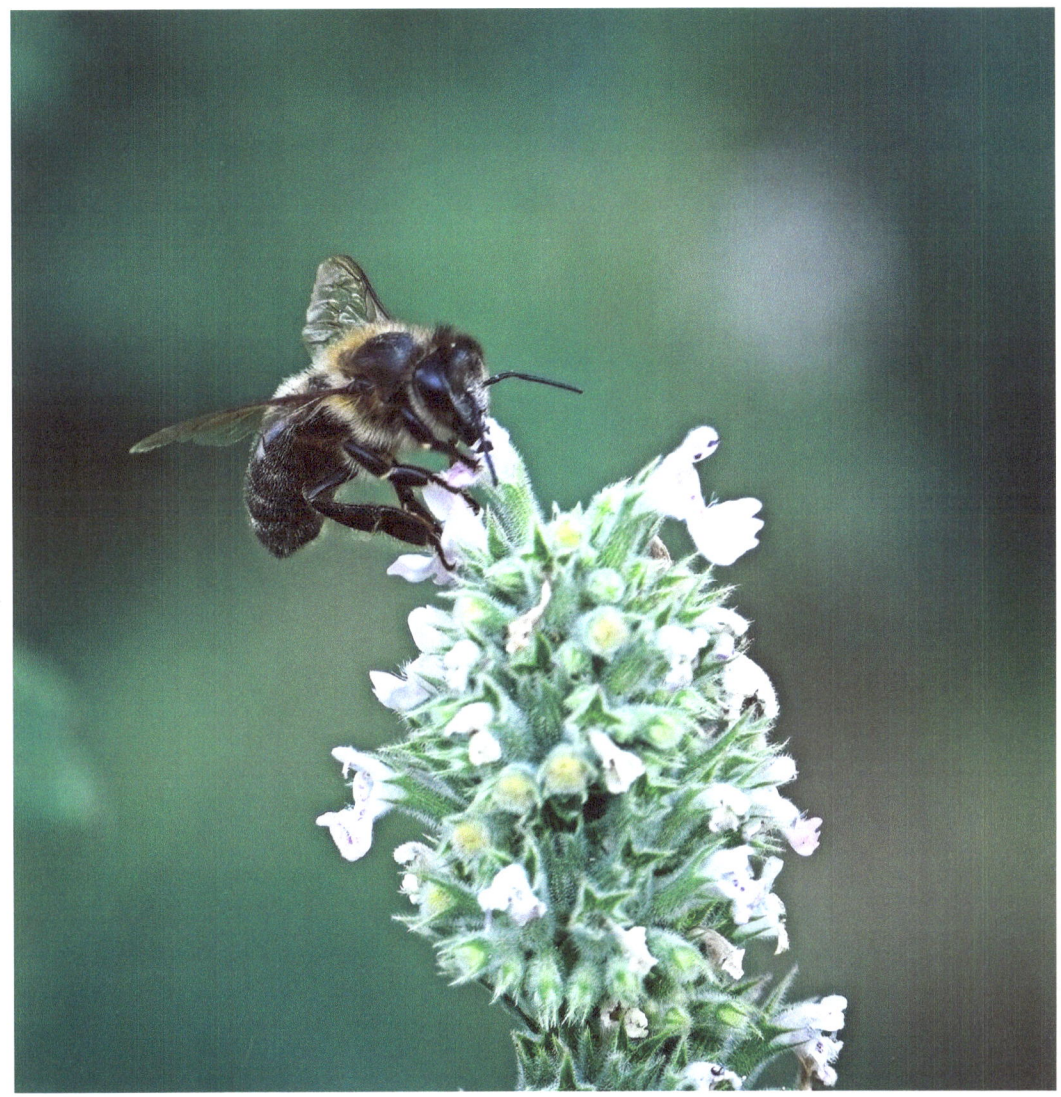

Honey Bee   *Jane Glesne*

Jane Glesne rediscovered photography in 1989. After years of compartmentalizing her life into education, fiber art (such as spinning, weaving and batik) or into nature study, she was thrilled to find one medium that could encompass her love of the earth, passion for texture and design, and her need to teach. Through her work, she hopes to encourage people to slow down and look more closely at the incredible natural world around them.

Living in Joseph, Oregon, she finds that the mysteries, delights and beauty of the area are endless. Her work has appeared in Adirondack Life, In Vermont Natural History, Healing Options and other publications.

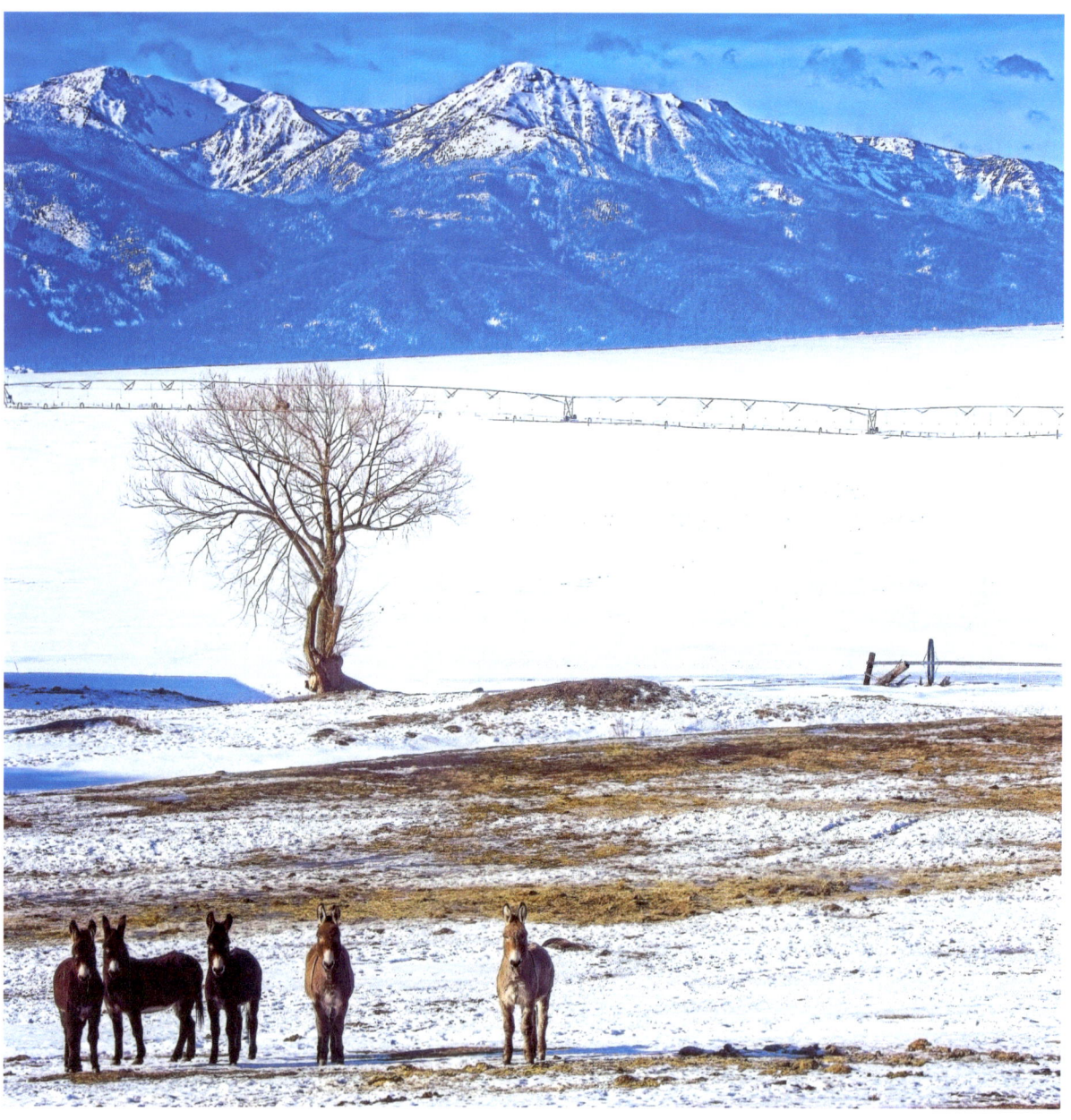

Did You Say "Carrot"?   *Jane Glesne*

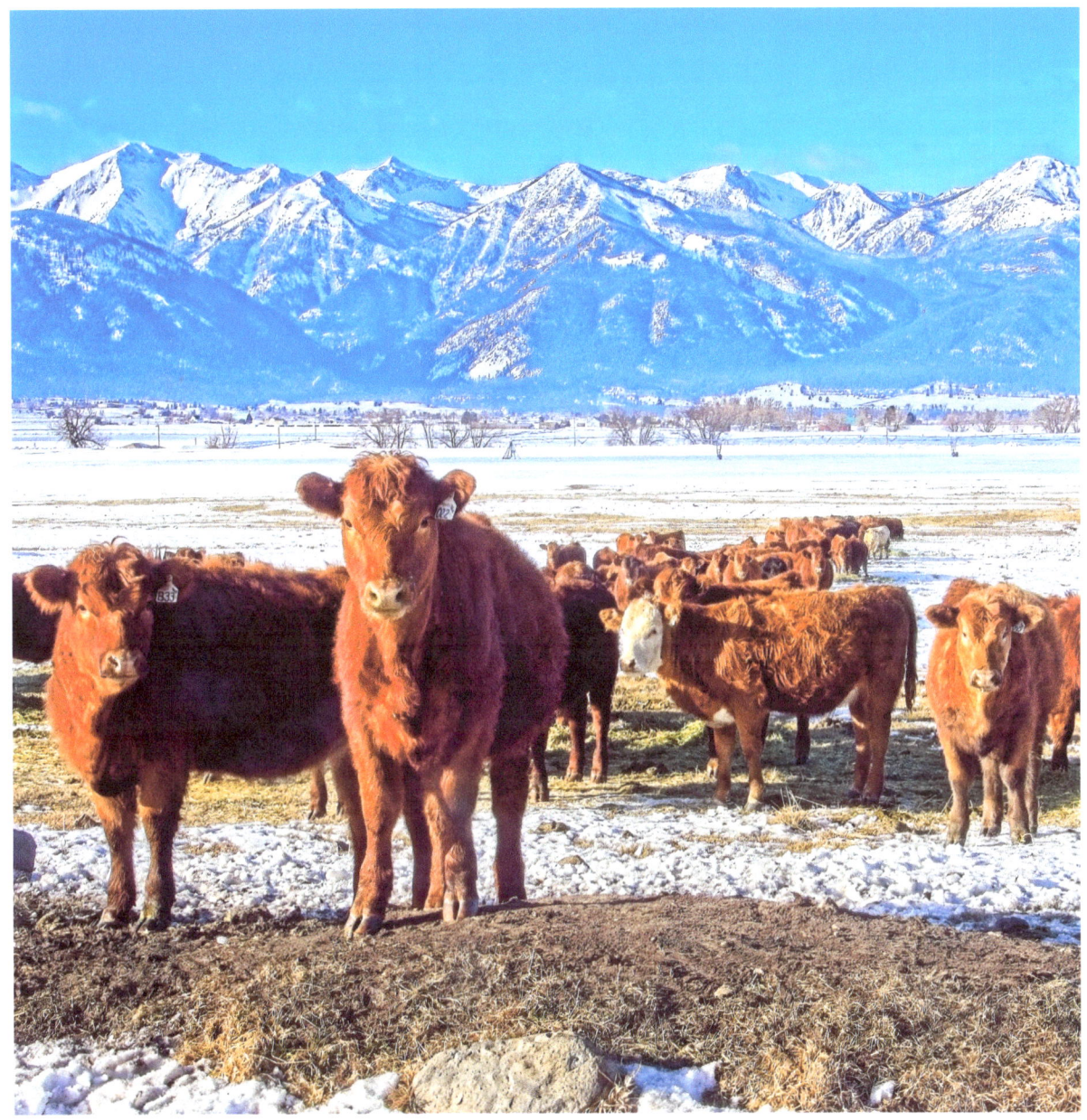

Winter Feeding   *Jane Glesne*

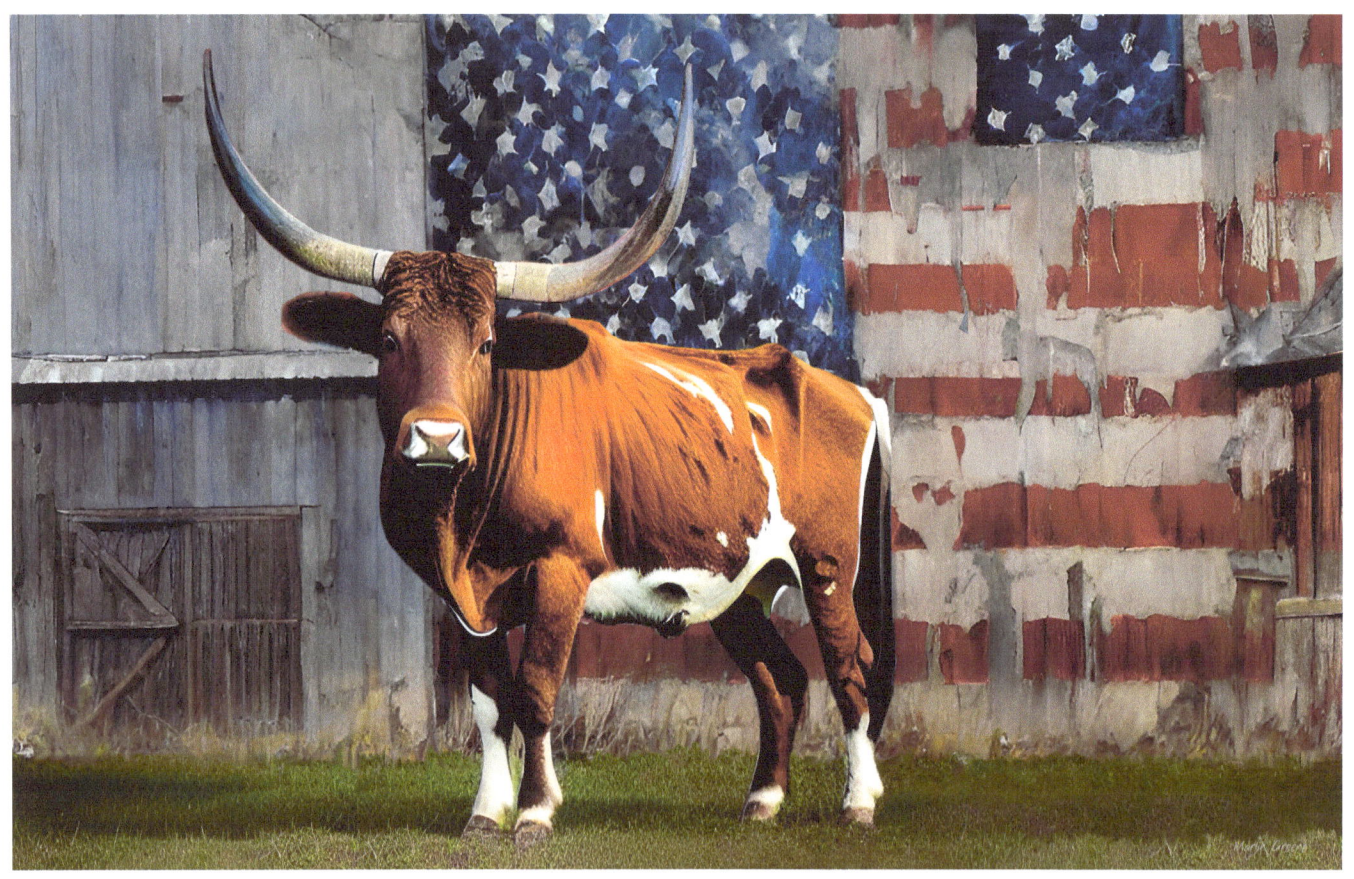

American Longhorn   *Marlin Greene*

My images are based on actual photos, AI generation and Photoshop. The result from the AI is
corrected and modified in Photoshop to achieve the desired final result you see here.
I hope you enjoy this new adventure in design and art.

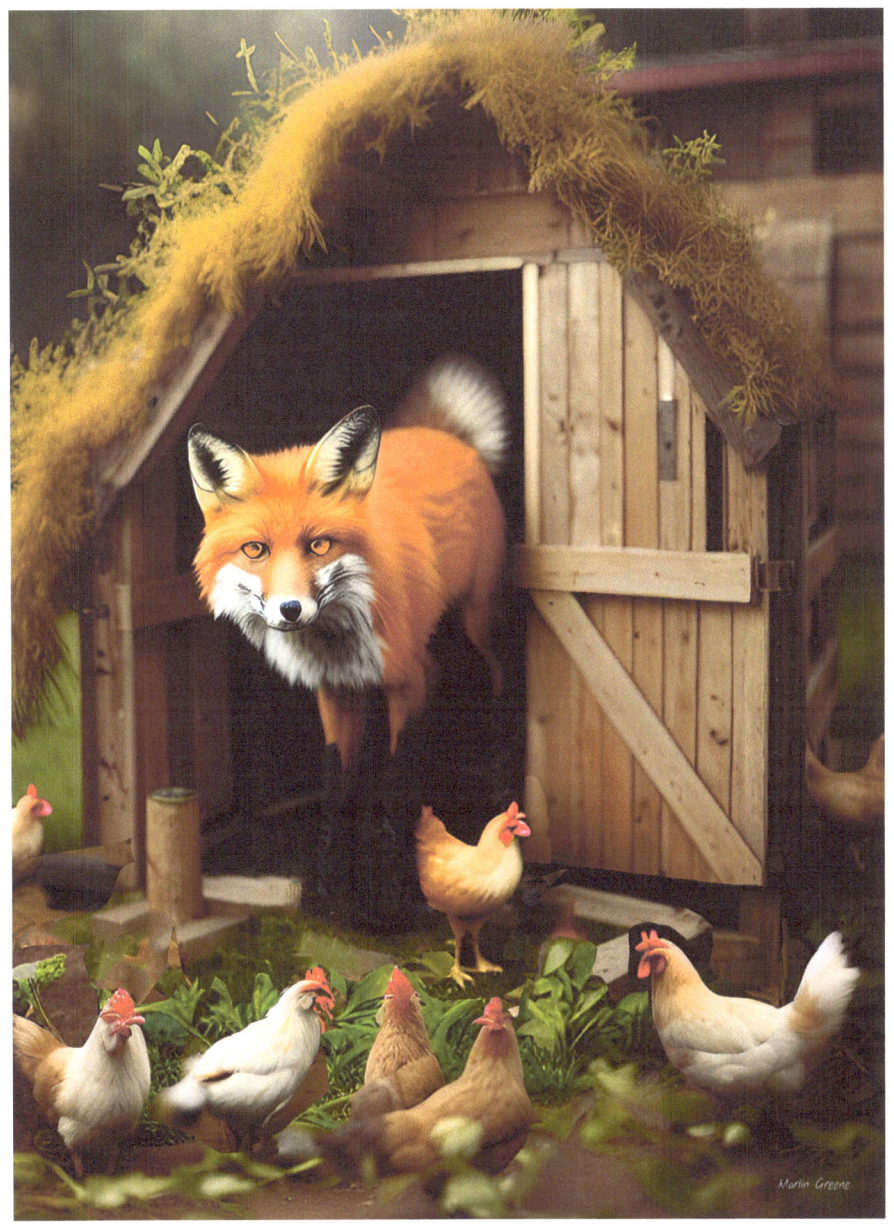

Oops   *Marlin Greene*

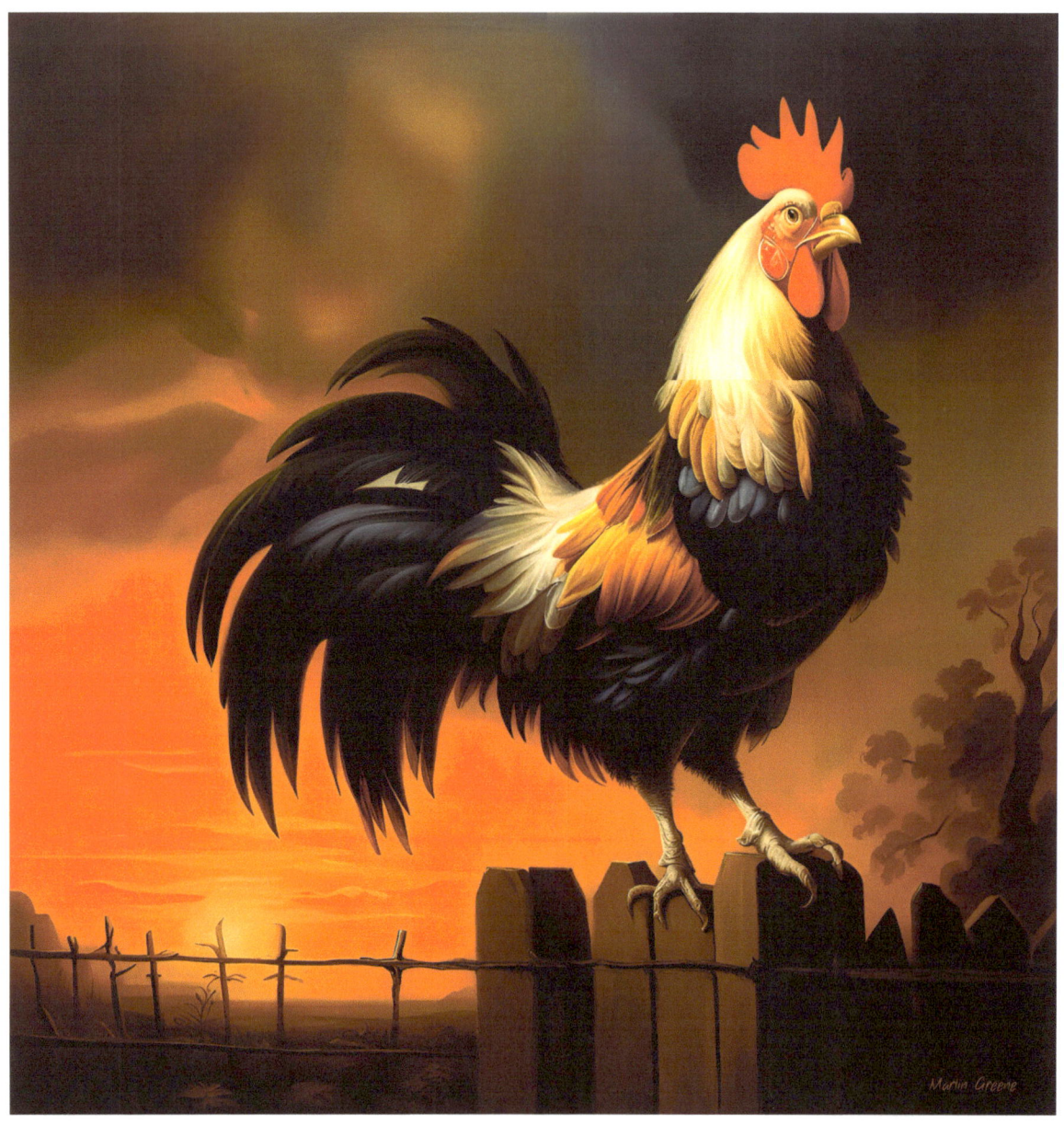

Good Morning   *Marlin Greene*

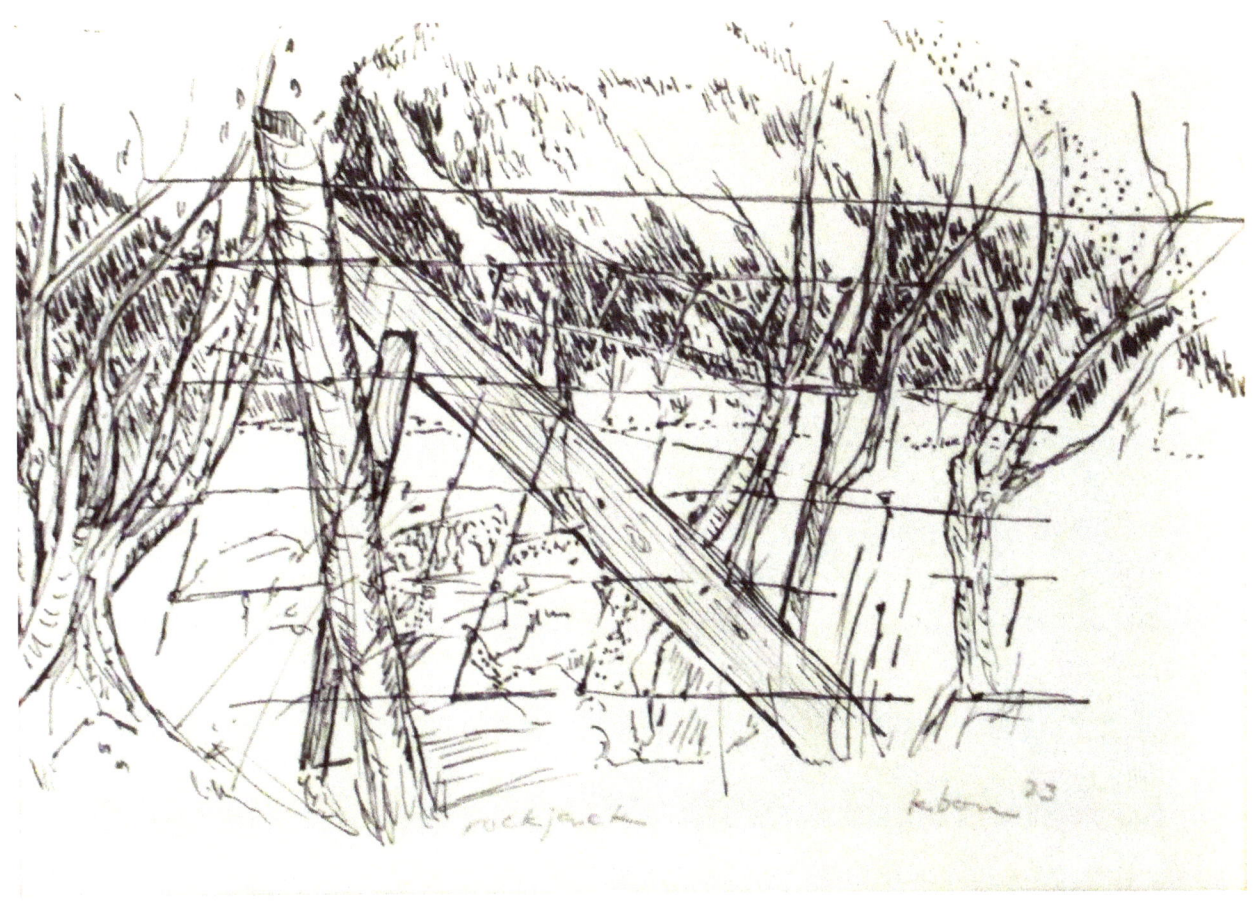

Rockjack At Triple Creek Ranch   *Kathy Bowman*

Kathy Bowman draws pictures, writes story poems and watches birds in Joseph, Oregon.

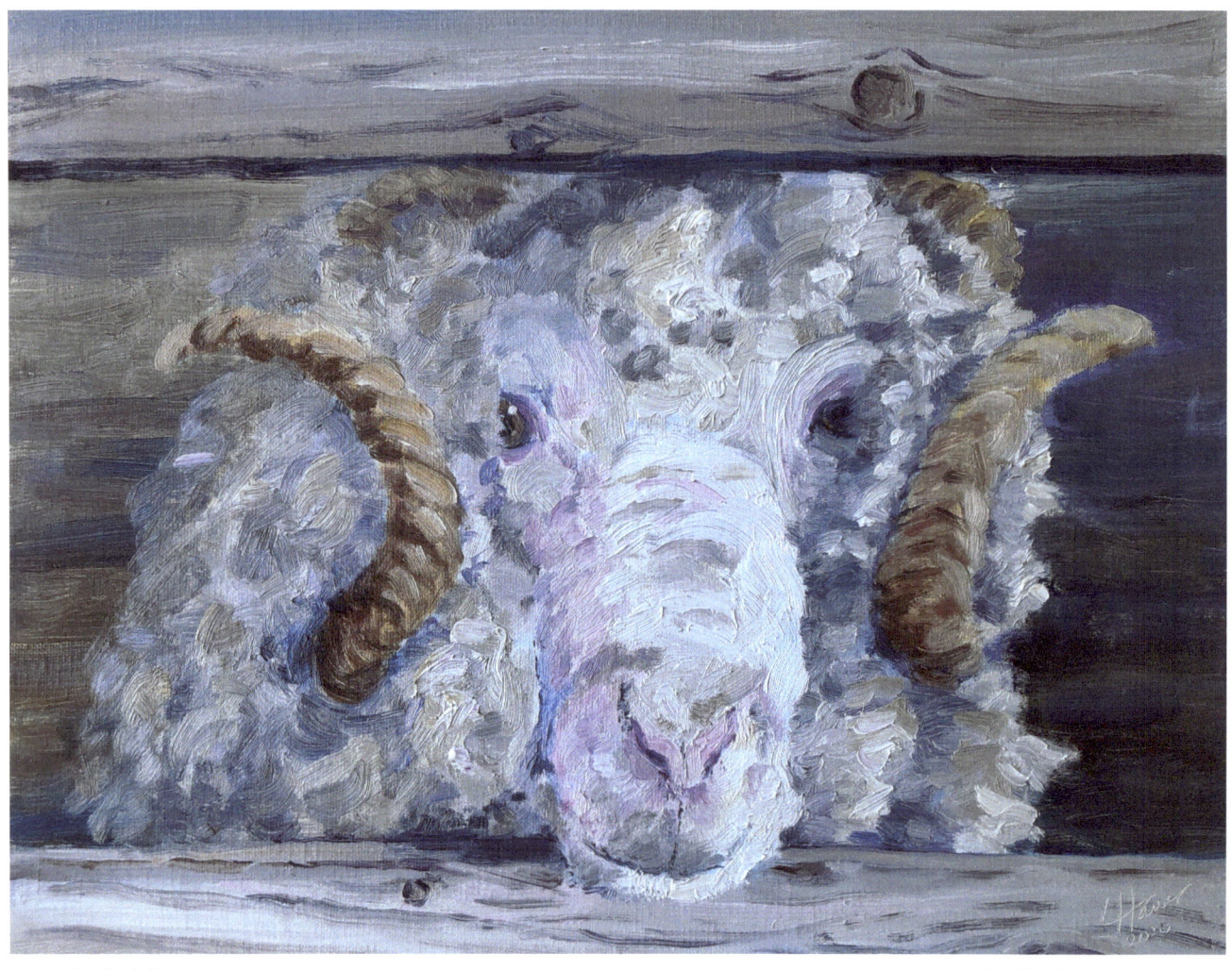

Peek-A-Baa   *Leslie Ann Hauer*

I returned to painting in 2015, after children, profession, and exploration of pottery and fiber arts. My love is painting, especially painting en plein air. I've been fortunate to have paintings selected for regional and national juried shows. And regardless of that, my intention is to continue trying to share 'moments' through my paintings!

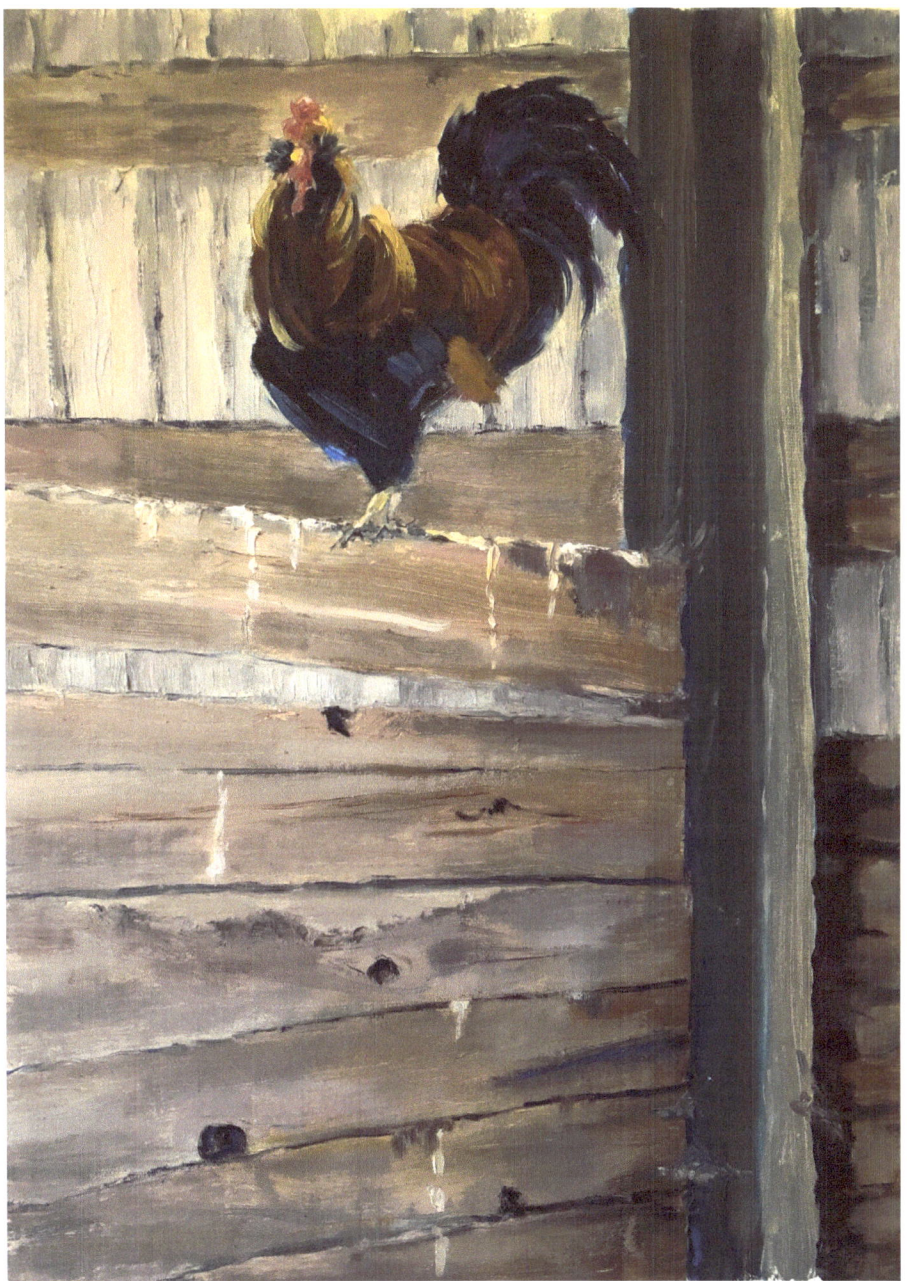

Fricasse? Who Said Fricasse?   Leslie Ann Hauer

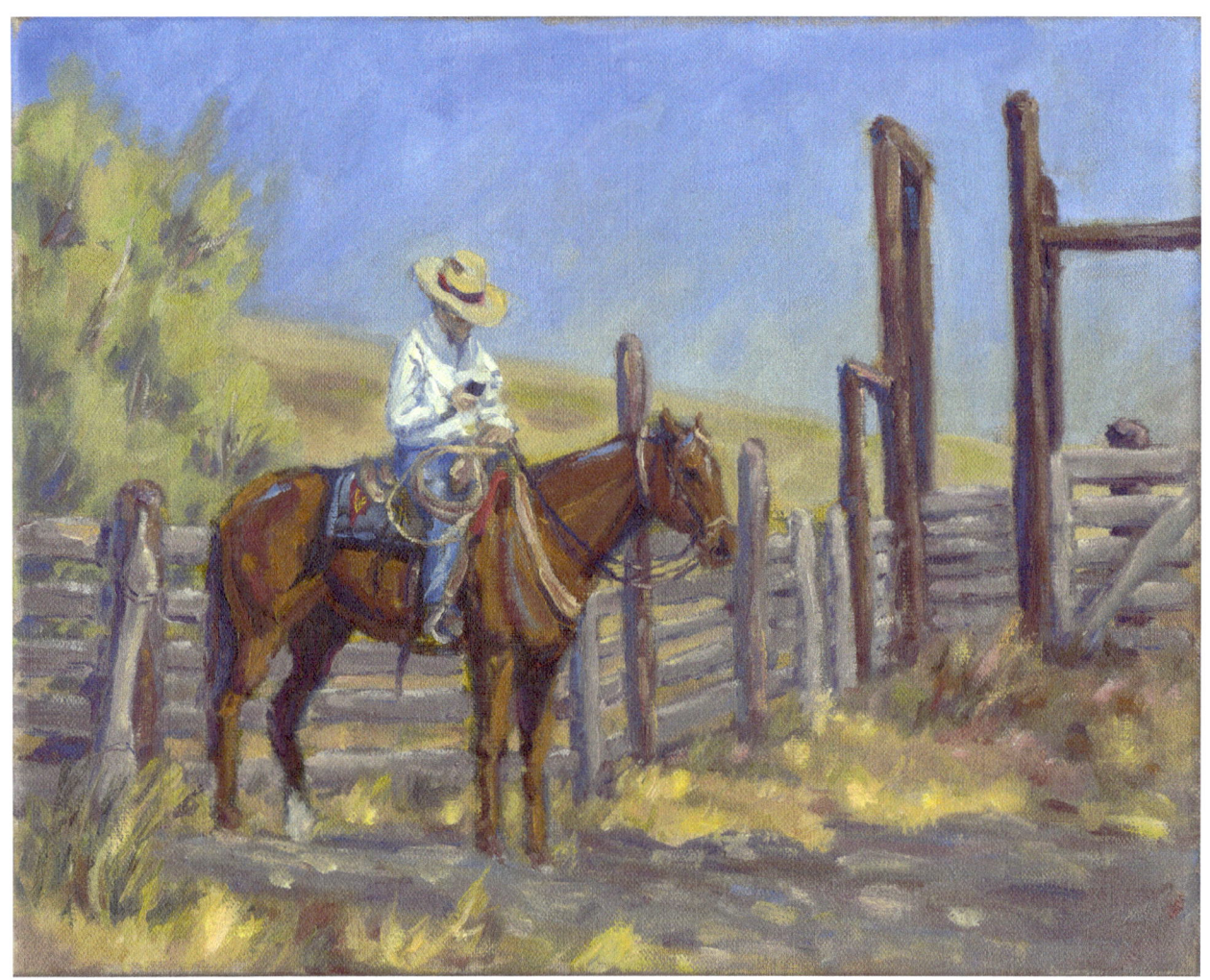

Checking The Mail   *Leslie Ann Hauer*

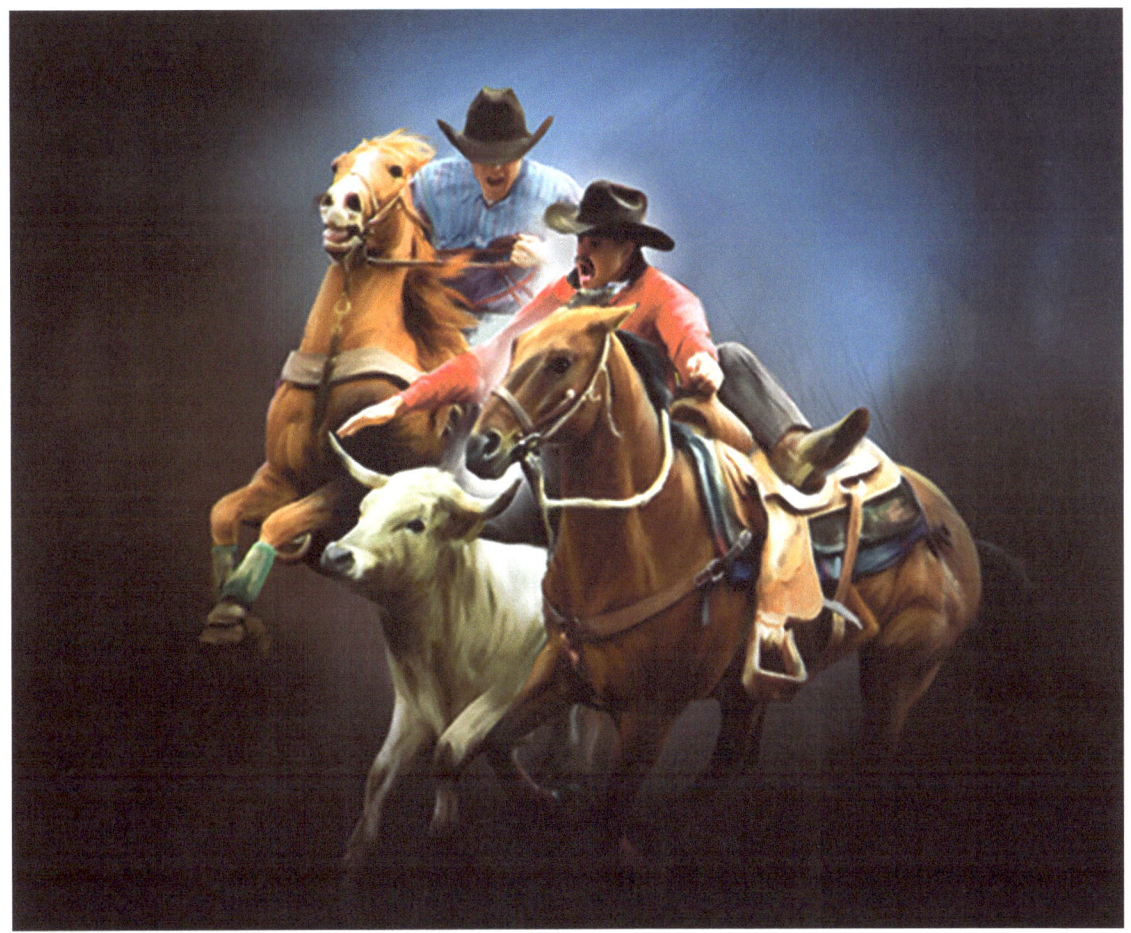

Steer Wrestler   *Judy Horn*

Judy Horn has been an artist as long as she can remember; painting and drawing have been her long-lasting passions. She loves to create images using all different media, including photography. Her photos are often taken with the creation of a new image in mind, and the subject in front of her camera will end up being a component in that image. Judy considers her work a success if there is an emotional and spiritual connection to the completed image.

Since attending Weber State in the mid 80's there have been many changes to art within digital media, and she has been there to see it all. In the 80's a semester's work was 3-4 images, now with scanners, printers and sophisticated electronic tools the creative process has become much more intuitive.

Judy is a Fellow PPW member and has earned degrees through the Professional Photographers of America: Master of Photography, Master of Electronic Imaging, Certified Professional Photographer and Photographic Craftsman. She has also won multiple photographic awards including National Loan Collection merits and Best of Show awards at the local, state and national level art shows.

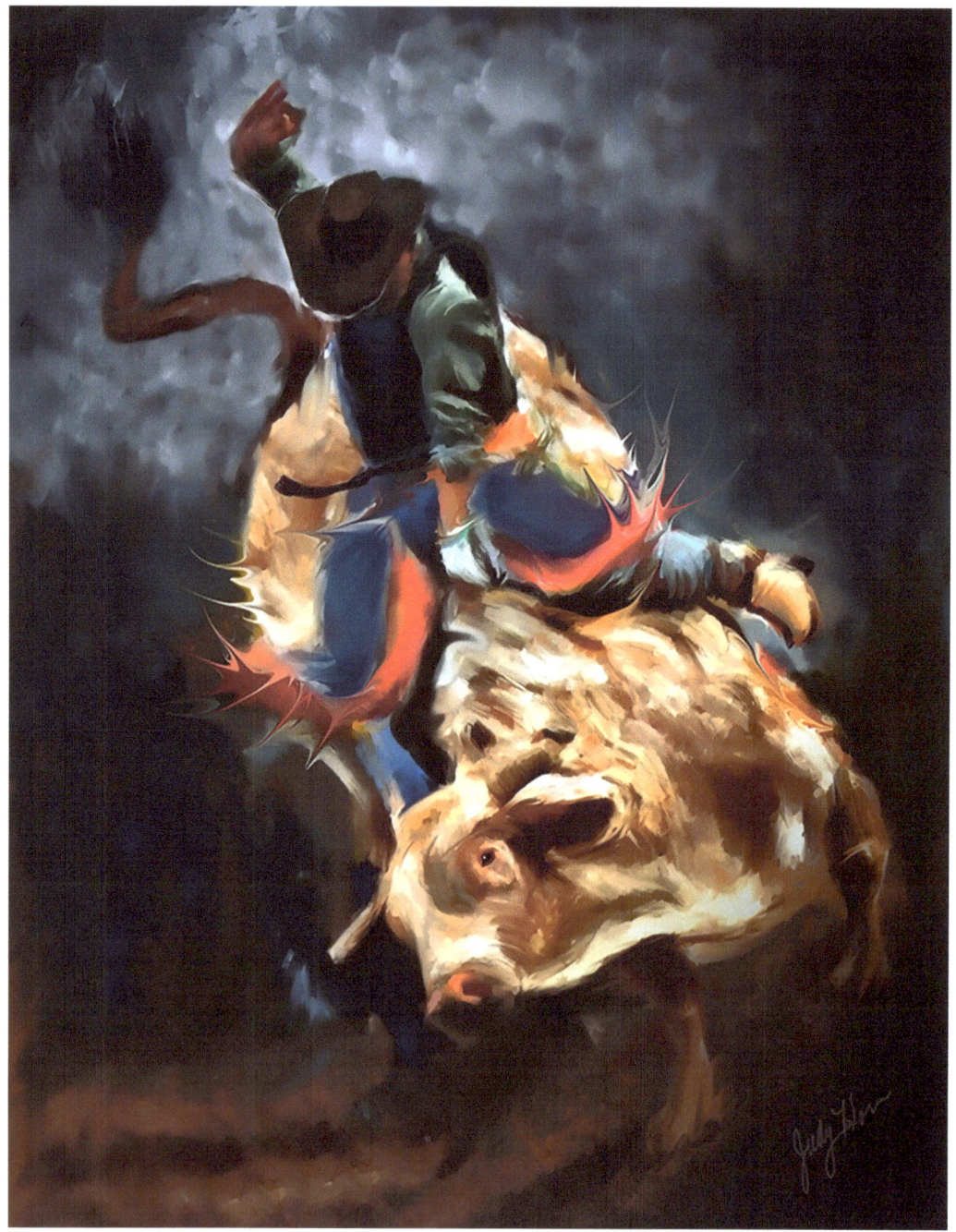

Eight Seconds of Terror   *Judy Horn*

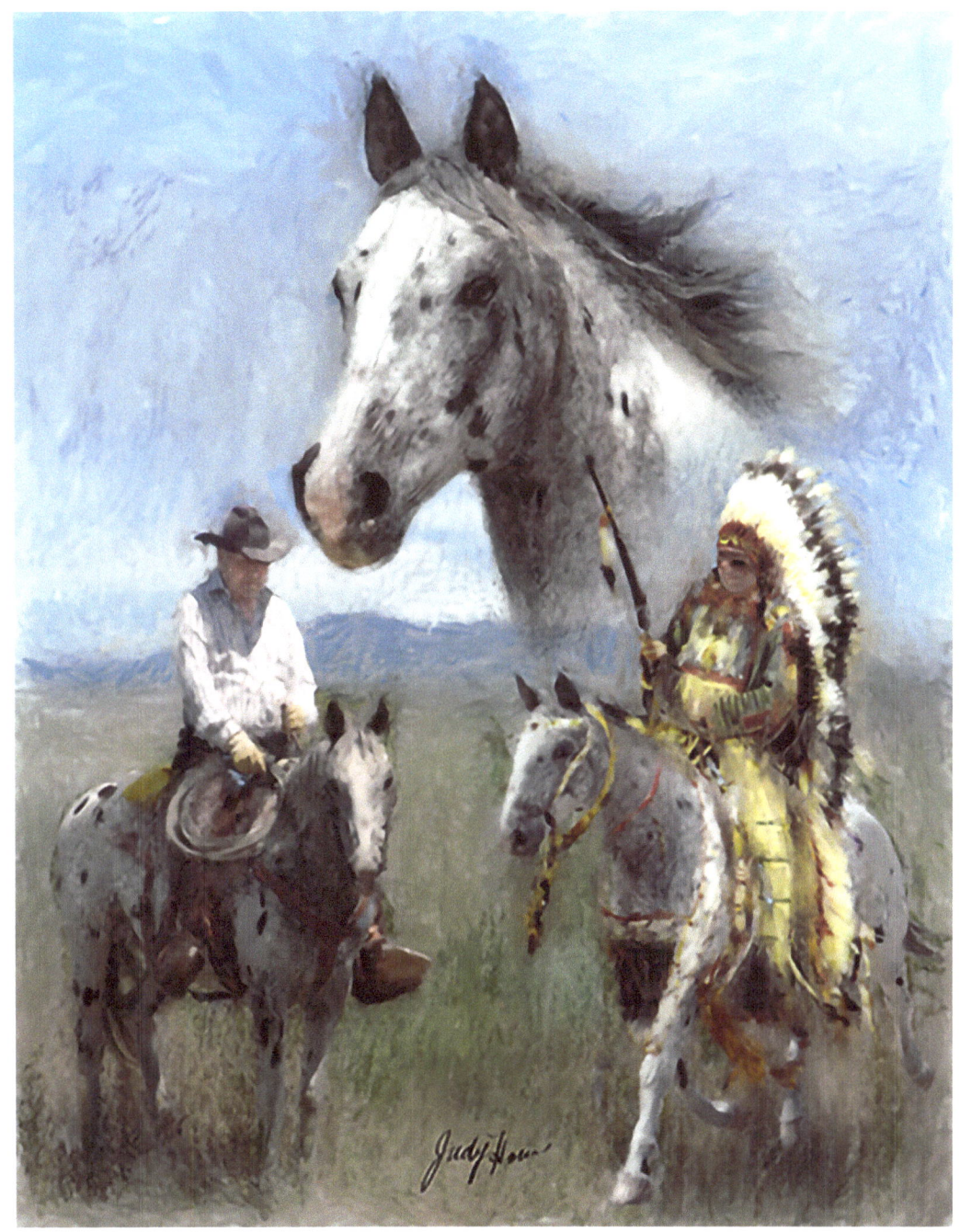

House of Two Cultures   *Judy Horn*

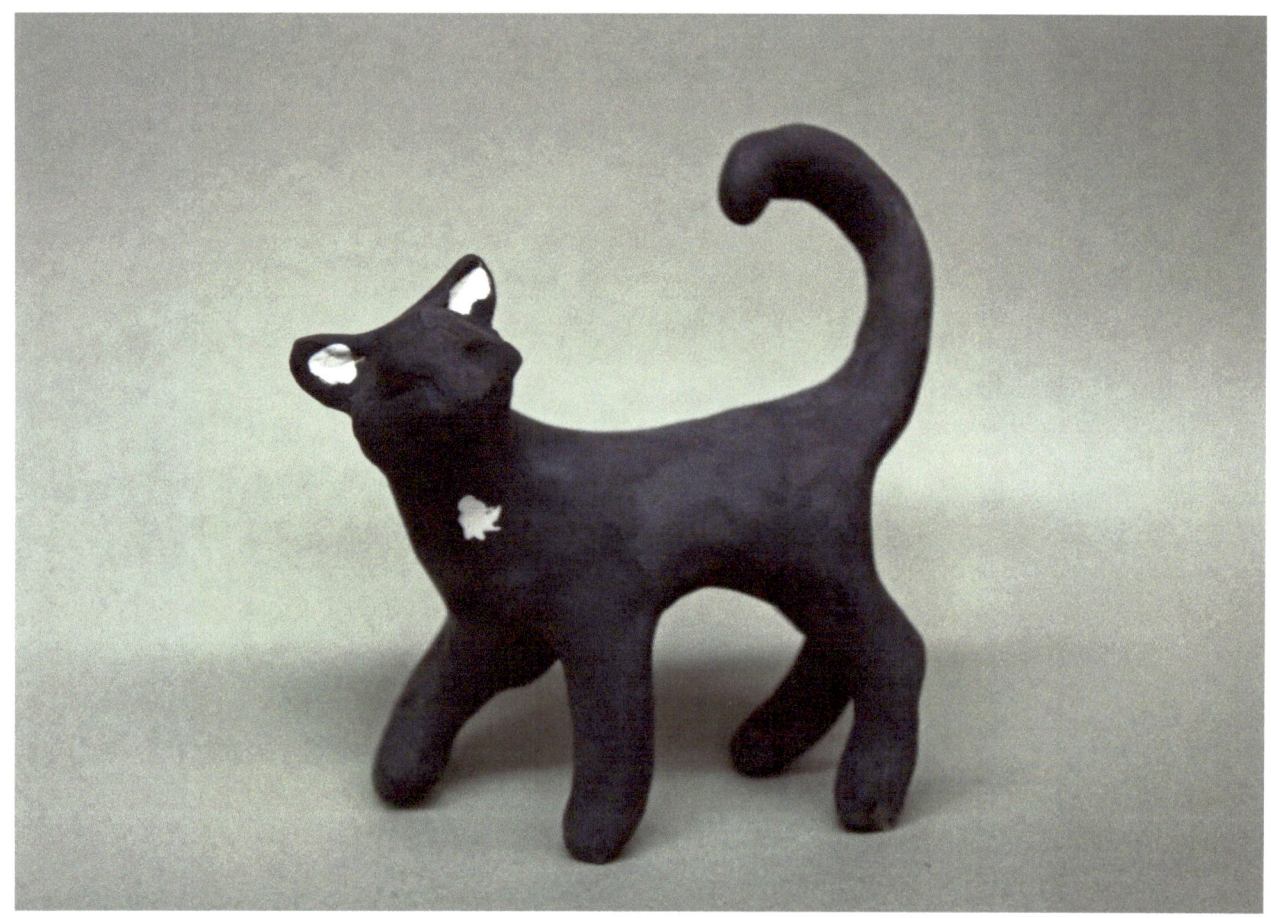

Rodent Patrol #1 Polly   *Jennifer Hawkins*

Our family valued all the 'Livestock' we raised. Especially dear to my father and myself were the many
Cats who kept the surrounding area rodent free protecting the crops, granaries, tack and home.

Jennifer Hawkins grew up on a working ranch of cattle, sheep and wheat in Northern Wallowa County, surrounded by
beauty, wildlife and dramatic landscapes, those experiences shaped her aesthetics.
Artist & Arts teacher, she teaches at Joseph Charter School, Troy, Imnaha and the Josephy Center.
Jennifer Hawkins holds BS, MS, MFA, from the University of Oregon.

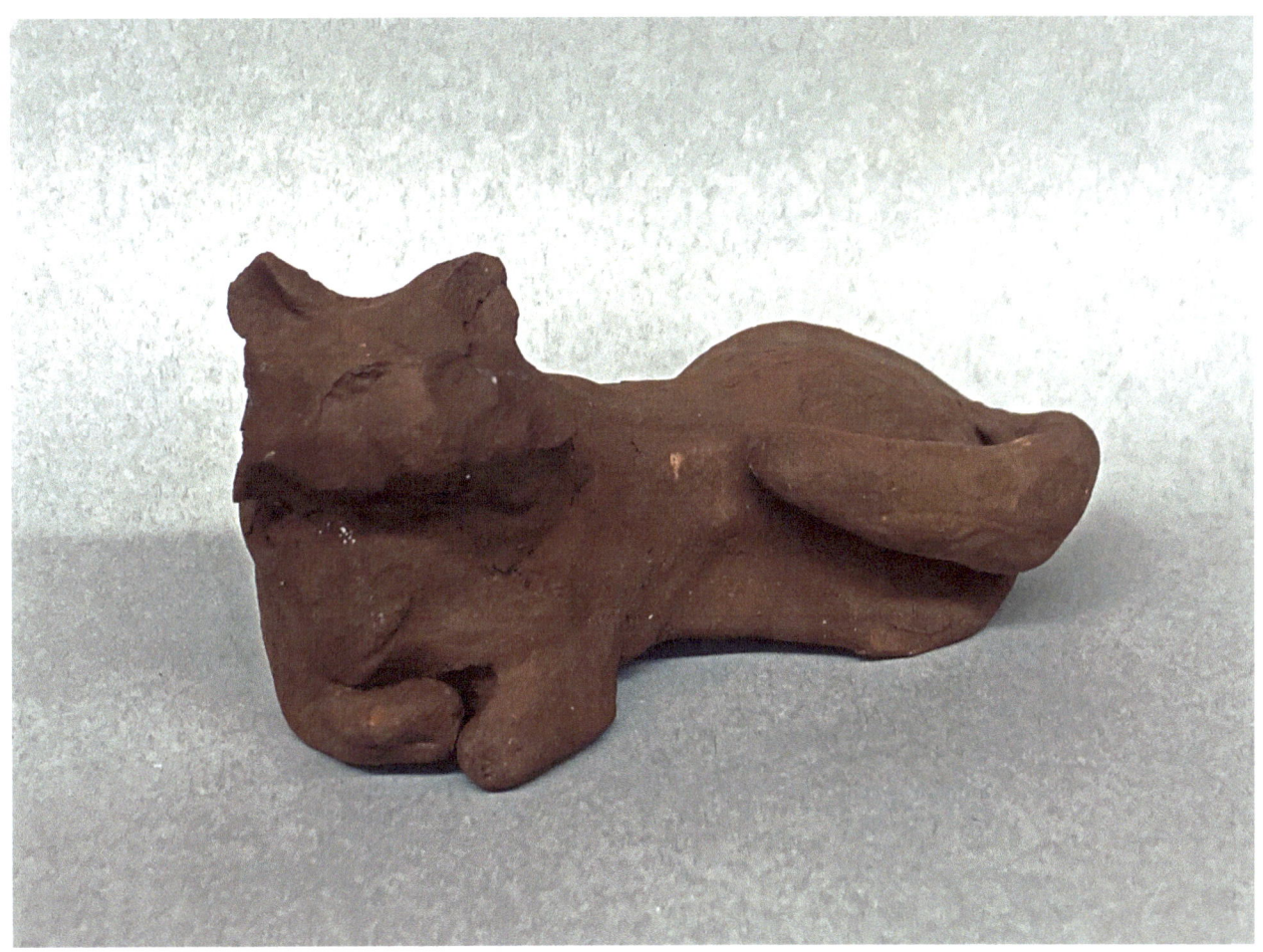

Break Time, Rodent Patrol #2 Hillary   *Jennifer Hawkins*

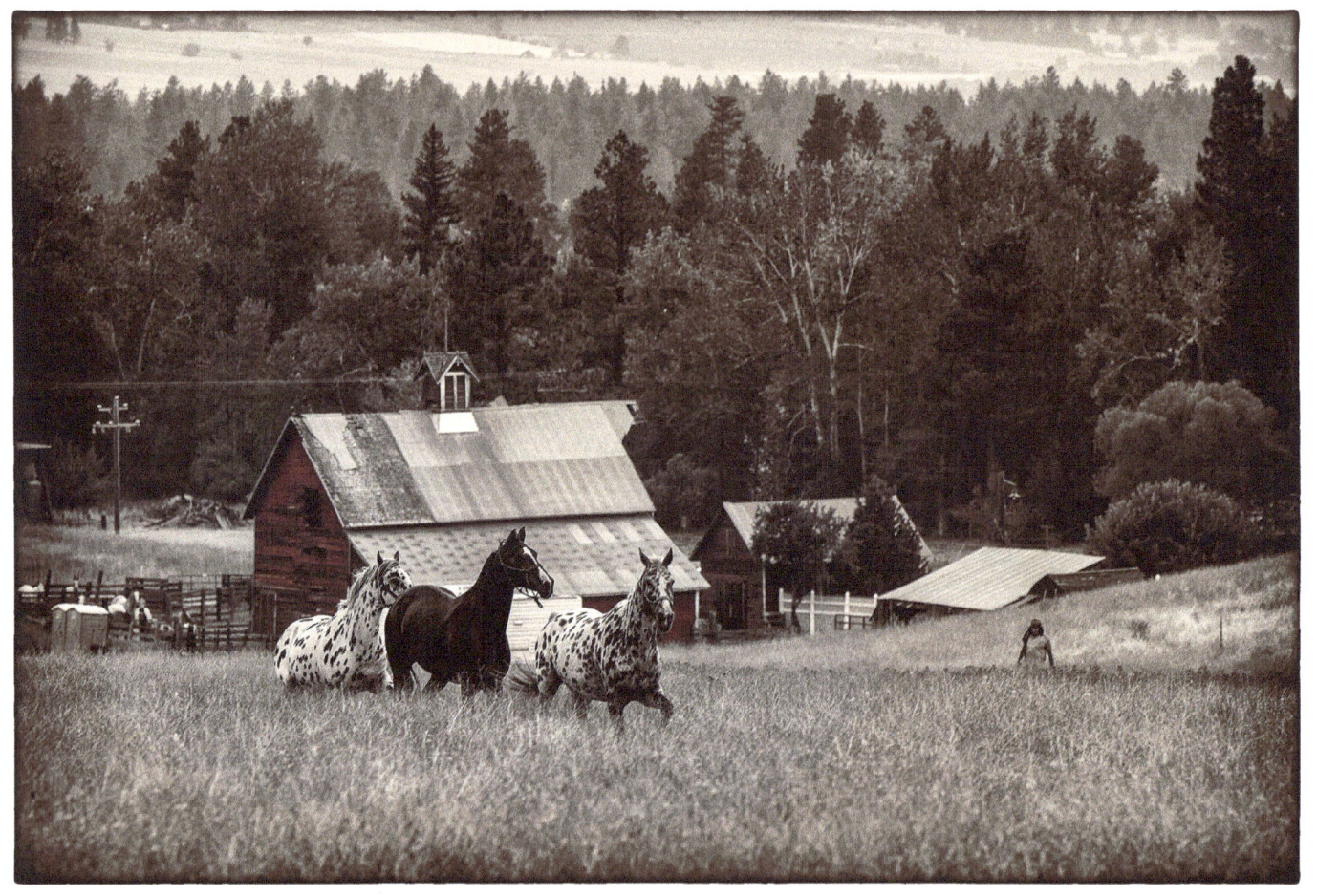

The Once & Future Herd   *Rob Kemp*

Photography and painting have been a lifelong passion of mine, while pursuing a career in graphic design.
My photos focus on travel photography, street photography, and architecture, the older the better.
I have shot in my Western US and many countries of Western Europe over 5 decades.

I often convert my photos to black and white. I am moved by the light and textures in
ordinary features of both urban and rural areas.

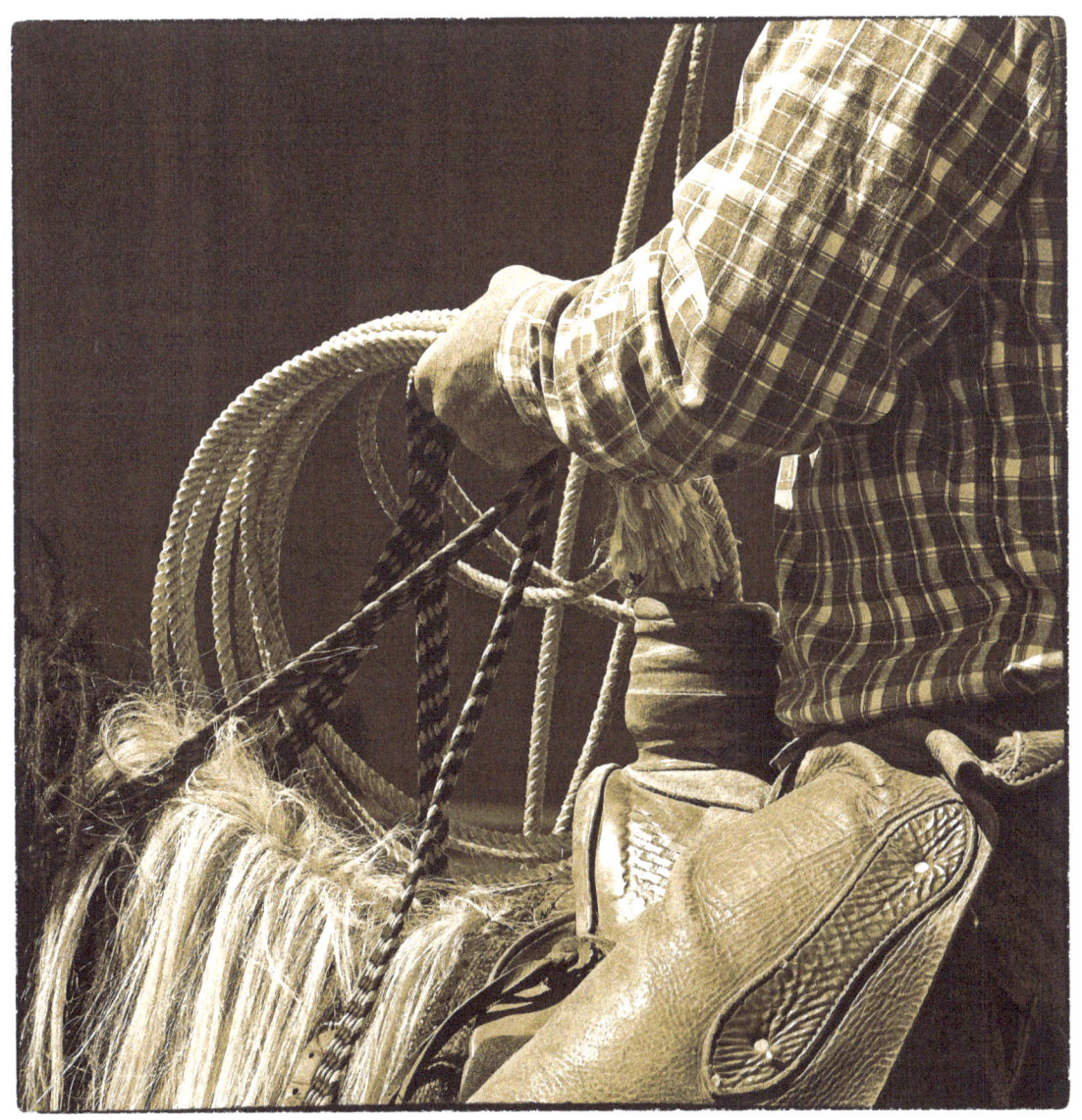

Tools Of The Trade   *Rob Kemp*

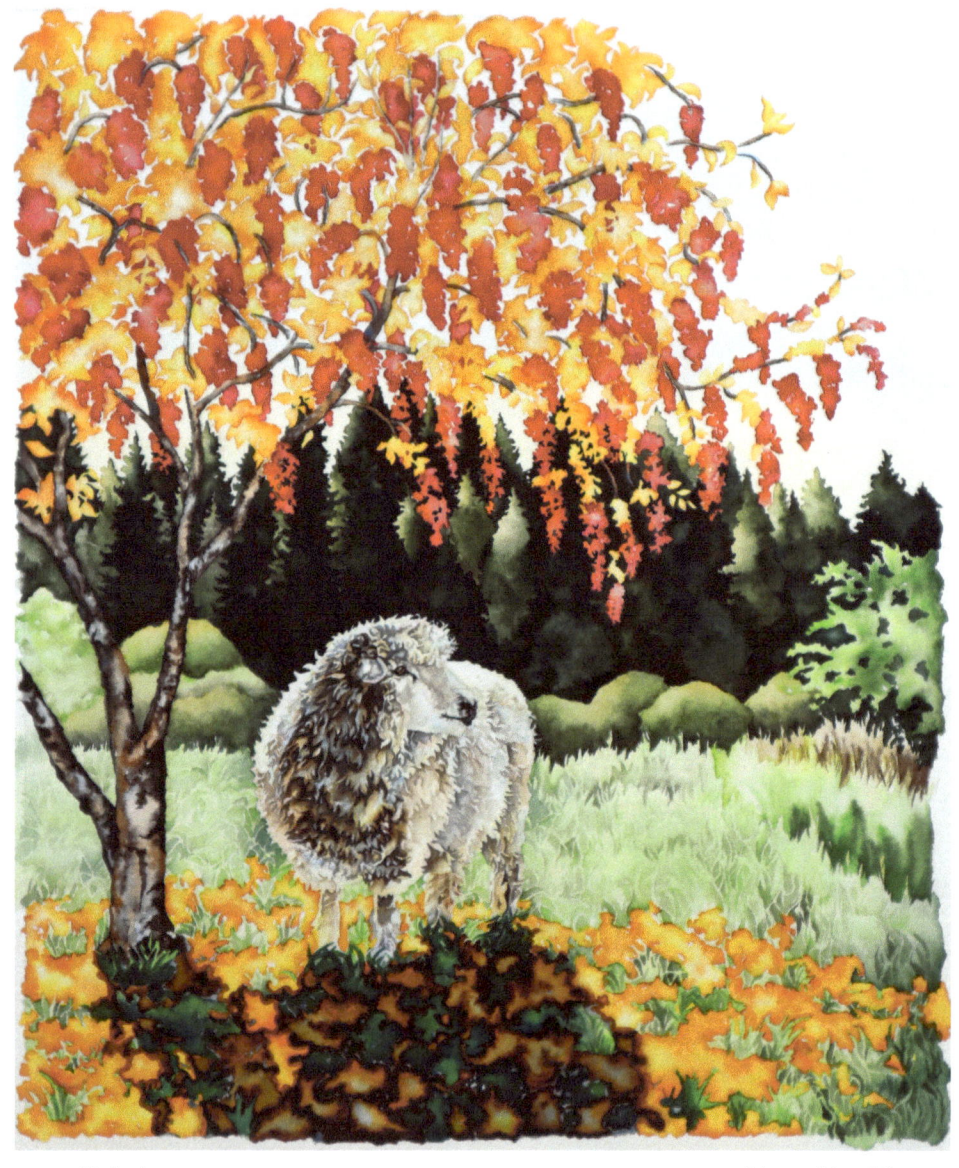

Melody   *Mary Aiwohi*

I am a veterinarian and artist living in Summerville, Oregon and I enjoy painting animals
and landscapes in translucent watercolor.

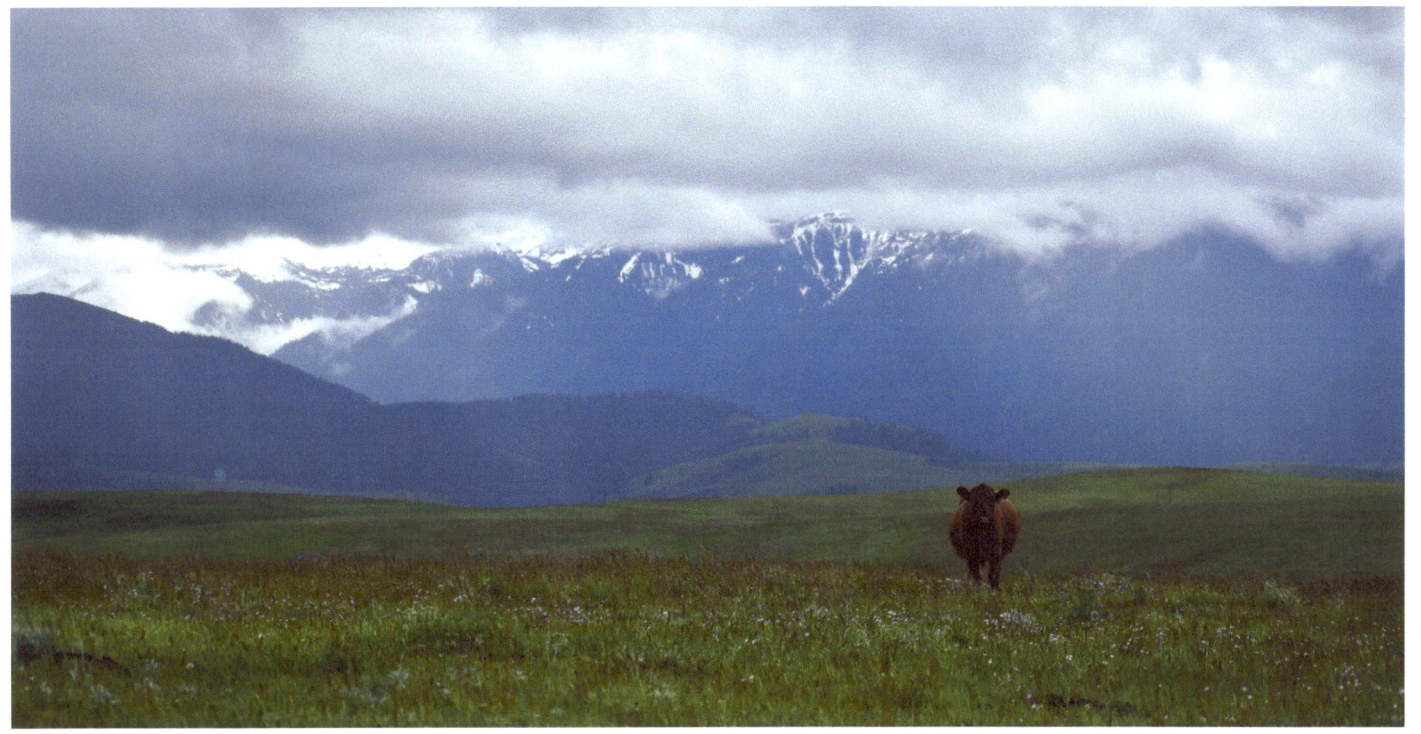

Mountain Cow   *Sadie Kennedy*

My husband and children and I live between Wallowa and Lostine and raise grassfed cattle. I am constantly inspired by the sounds, smells, textures, and sights of our cattle and farm animals. These animals nourish not only our bodies through high quality nutritious animal products, but also in the richness they add to our daily lives. My intention is to capture the feeling of life on our farm in a still image. In a time where it seems so many seek to devalue traditional meat in favor of heavily processed manufactured foods, it is more important to me than ever to shine a light on the simple beauty of raising good food.

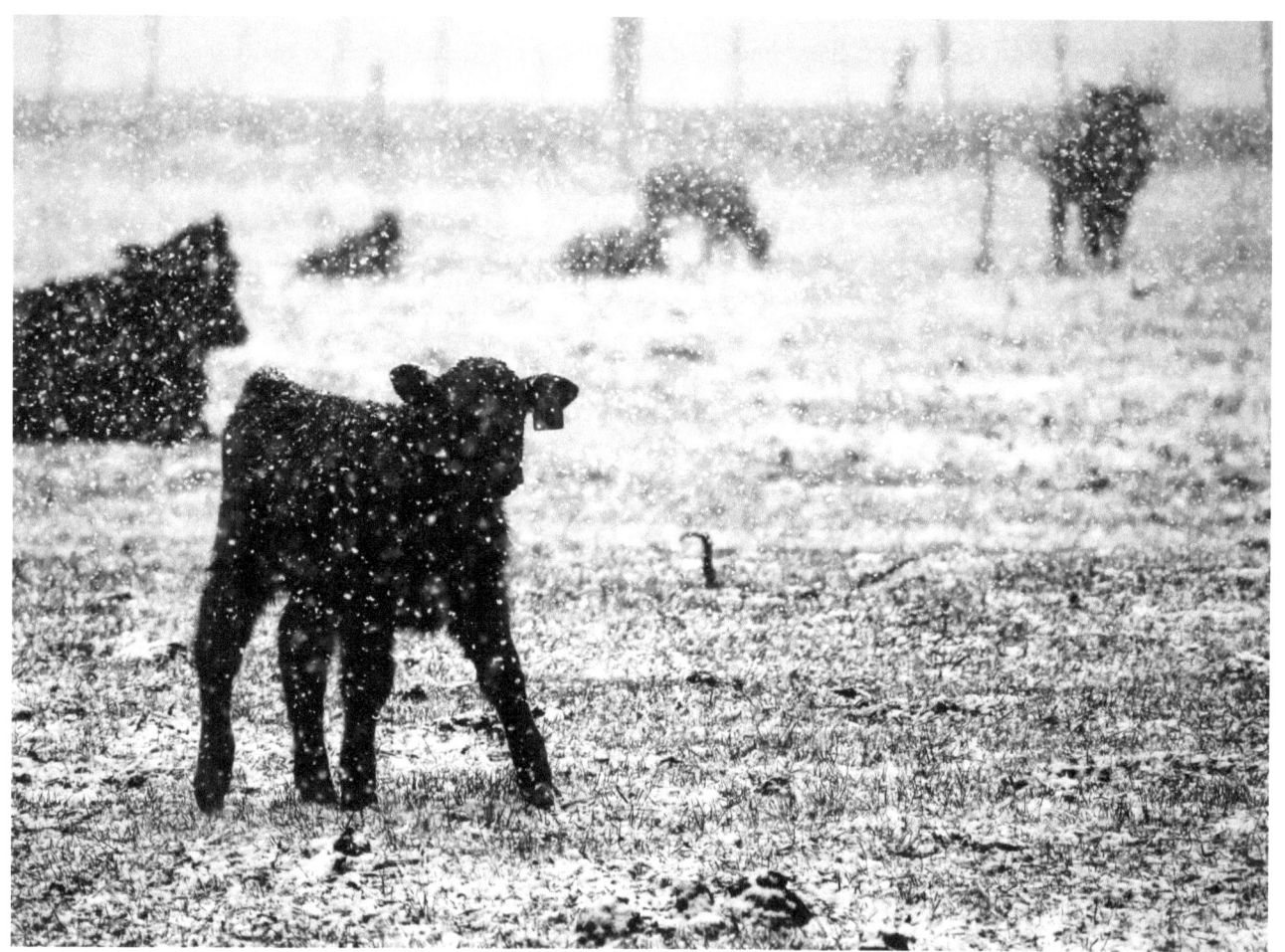

Wallowa County Spring   *Sadie Kennedy*

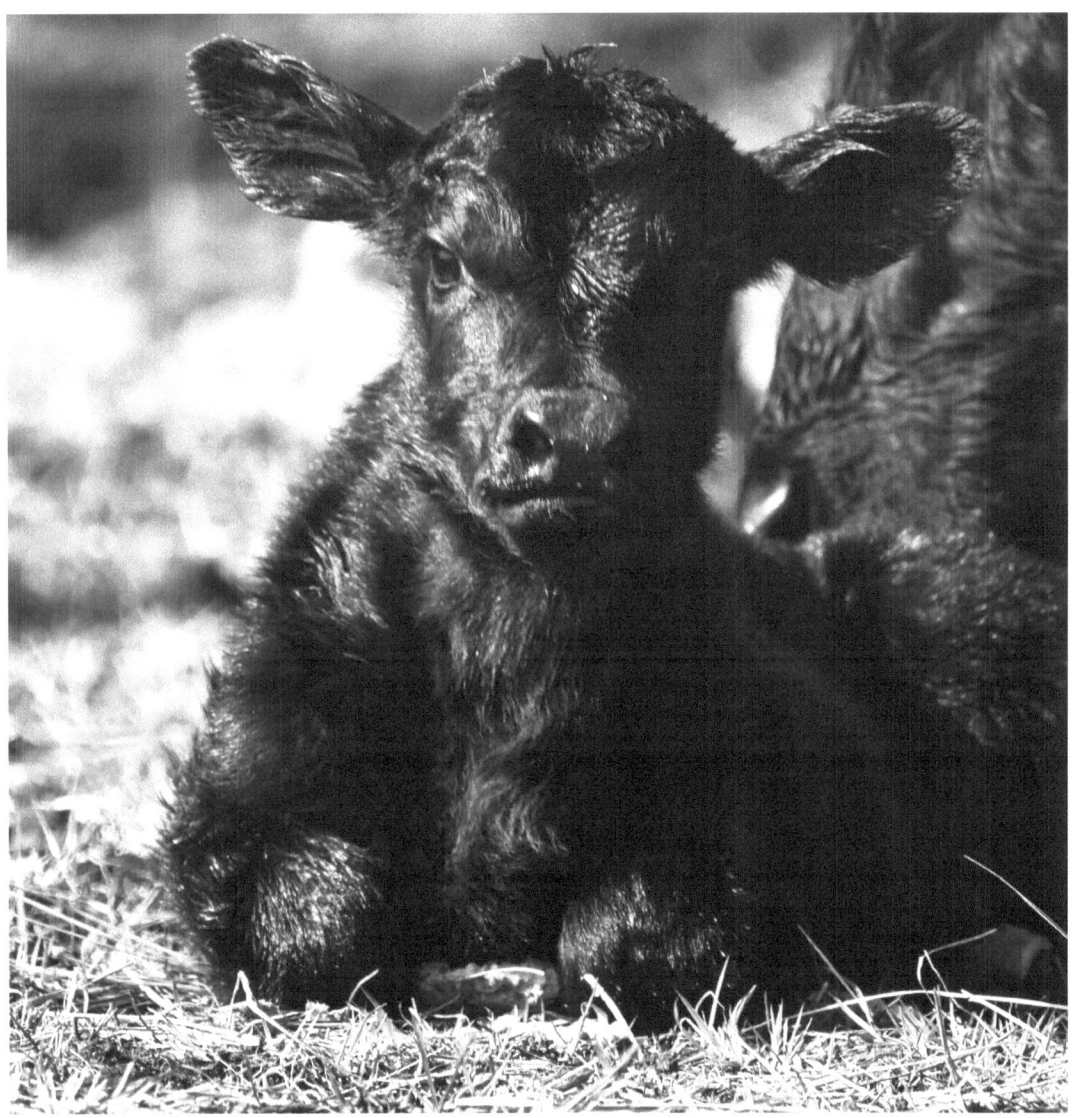

New Angus Calf   *Sadie Kennedy*

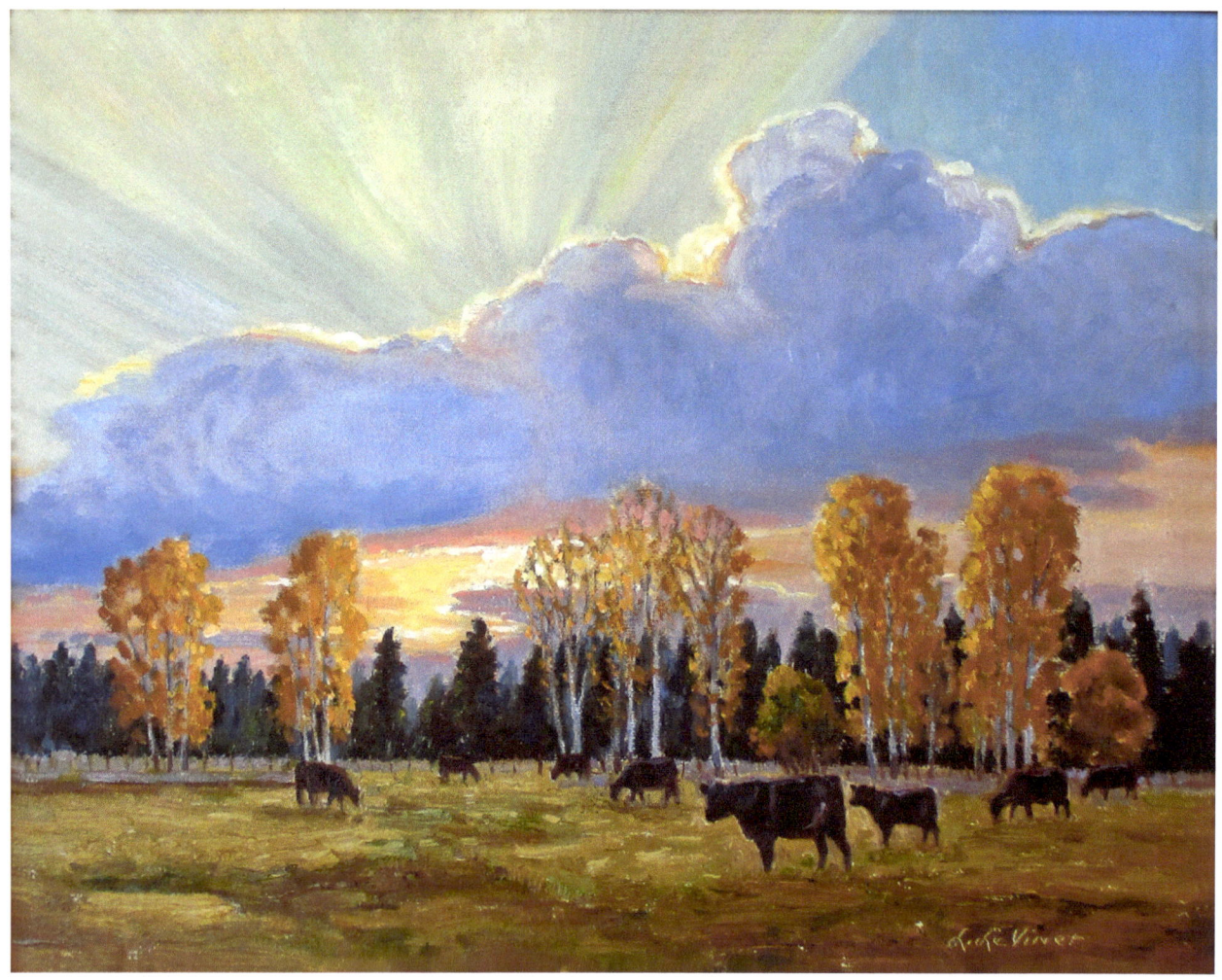

Sunburst & Cows   *Leslie LeViner*

Leslie LeViner, en plein air painter, lives on a ranch in Wallowa Valley.

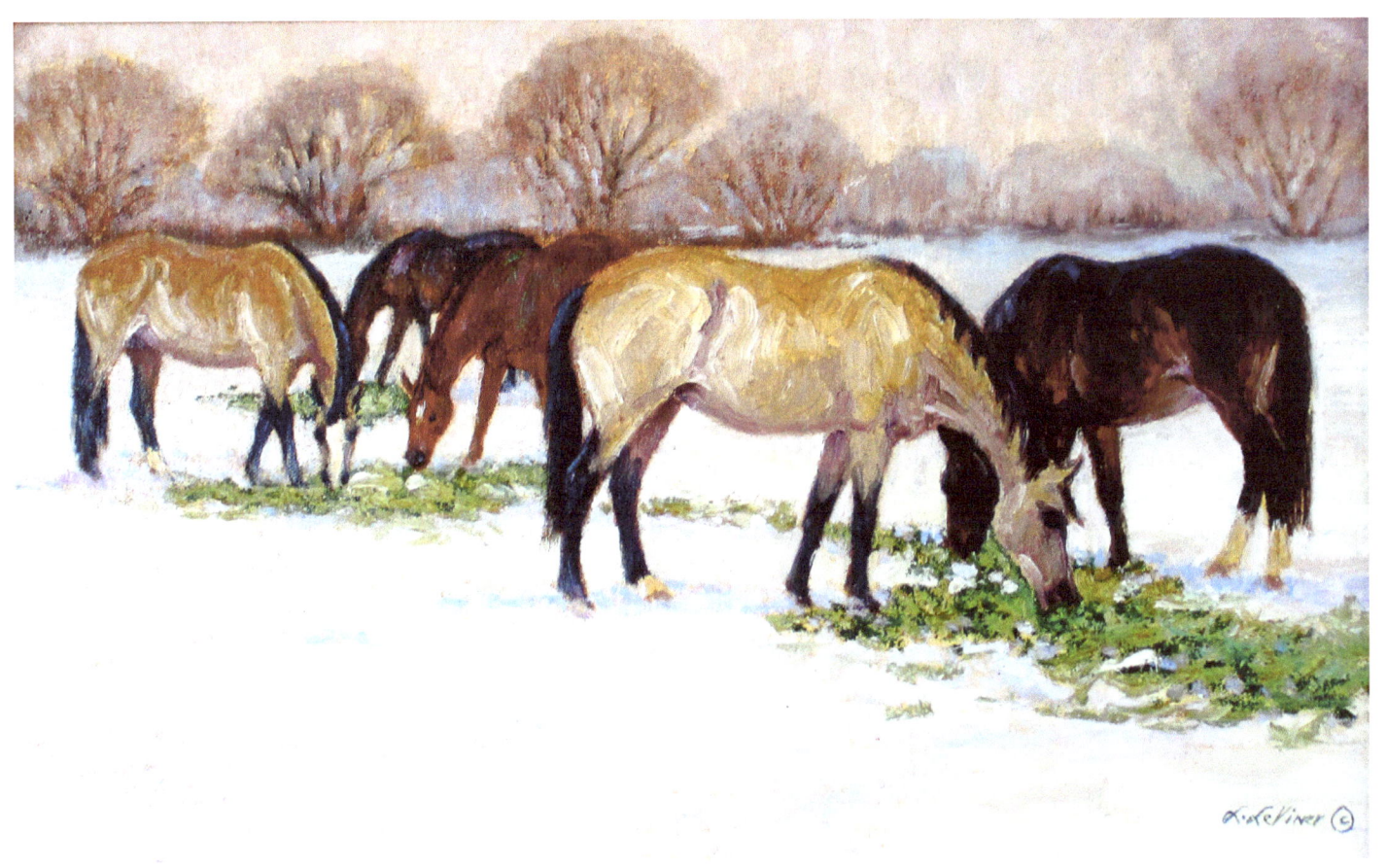

Buckskin Sisters   *Leslie LeViner*

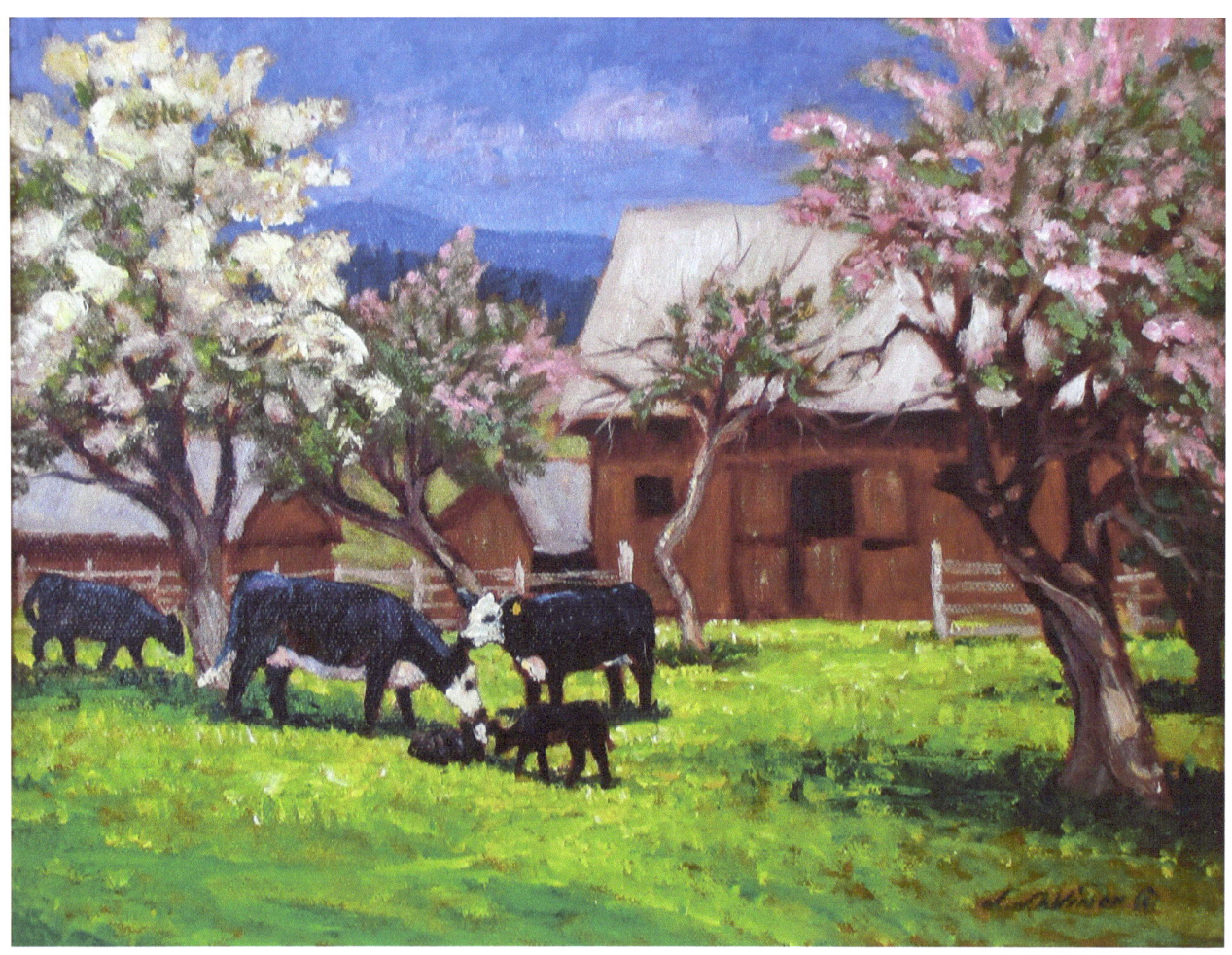

Cows & Calves in Orchard   Leslie LeViner

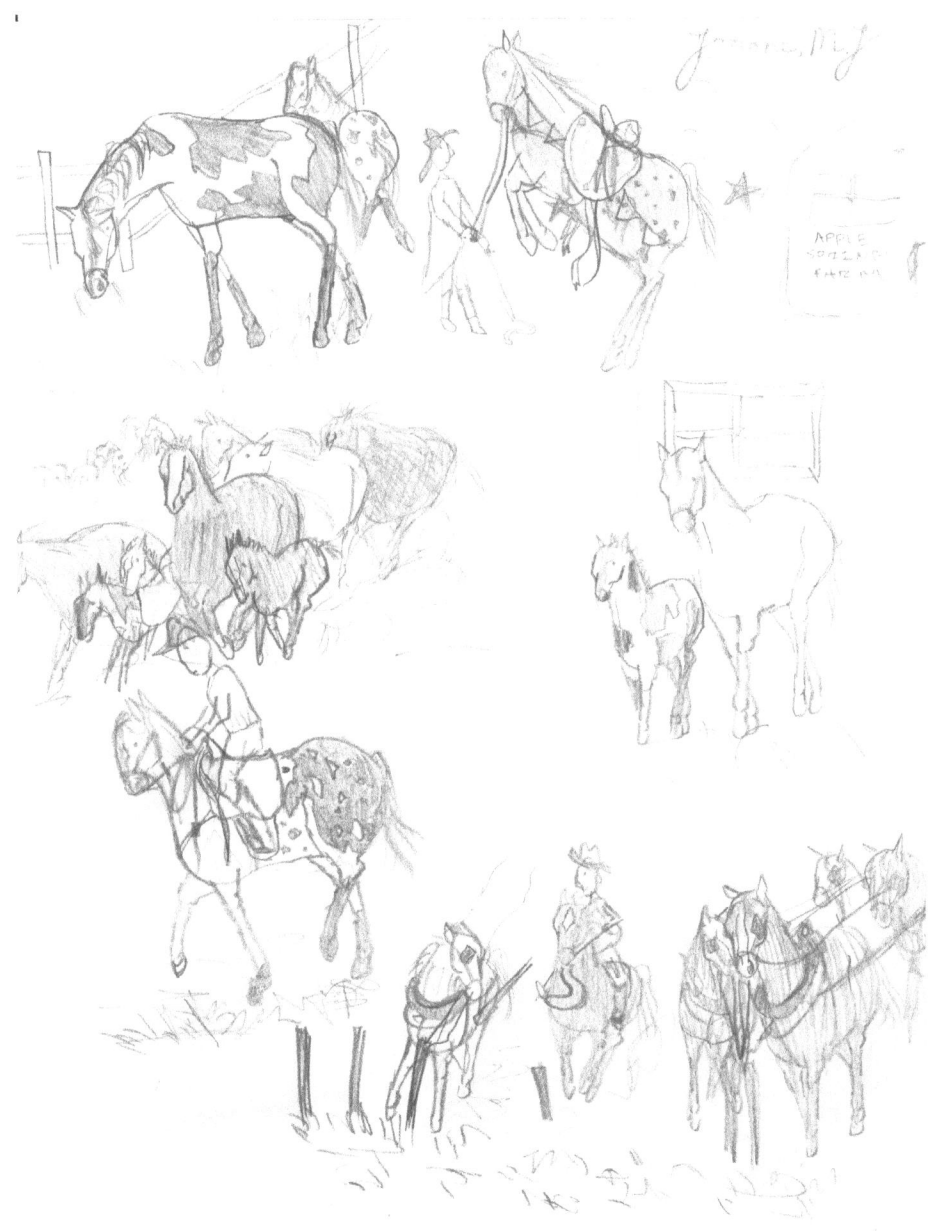

Horses At Show, Work, And In The Wild   *Lorane Lingard*

Lorane is a 3rd grader at Enterprise Elementary.

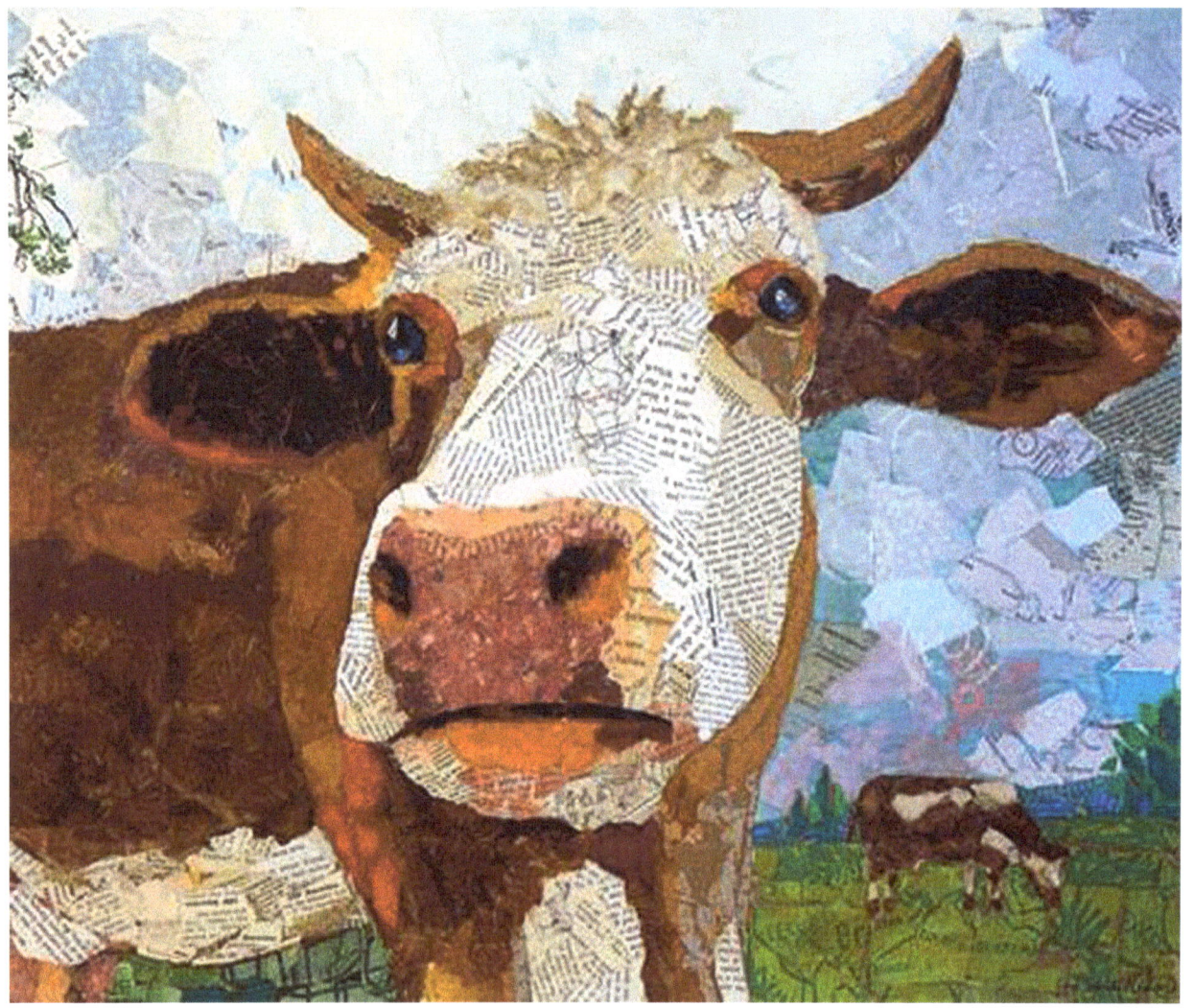

Cow On The Farm   *Susan Mcclellan*

Susan Mcclellan is a collage and watercolor artist living in Pittsburgh. PA. She is a member of the North Hills Art Center and Pittsburgh Collage Collective. Her work has been sold in libraries, craft shows, and art auctions. She also frequently donates her work to non-profits for their fundraisers.

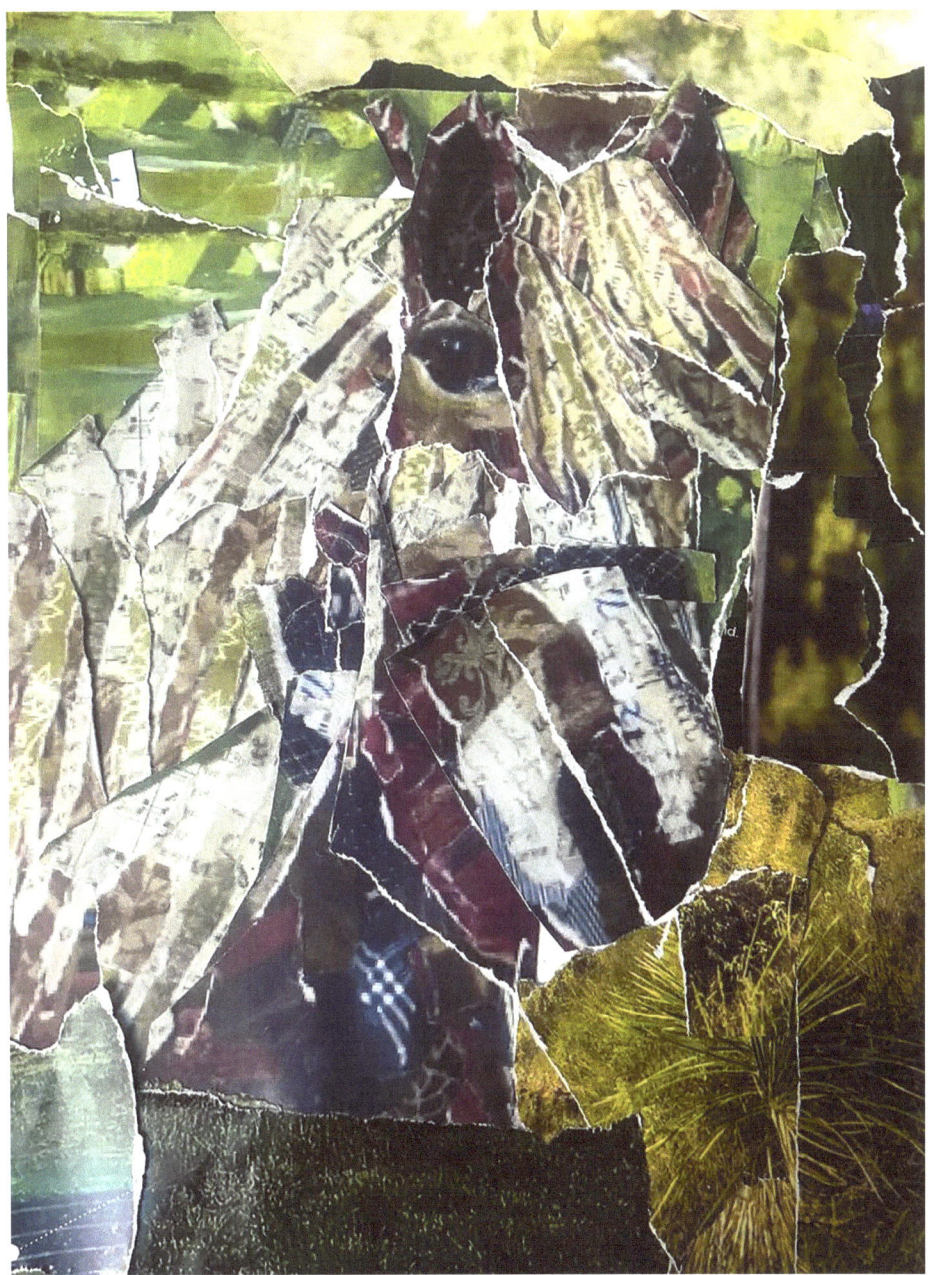

Horse Silhouette Collage   *Susan Mcclellan*

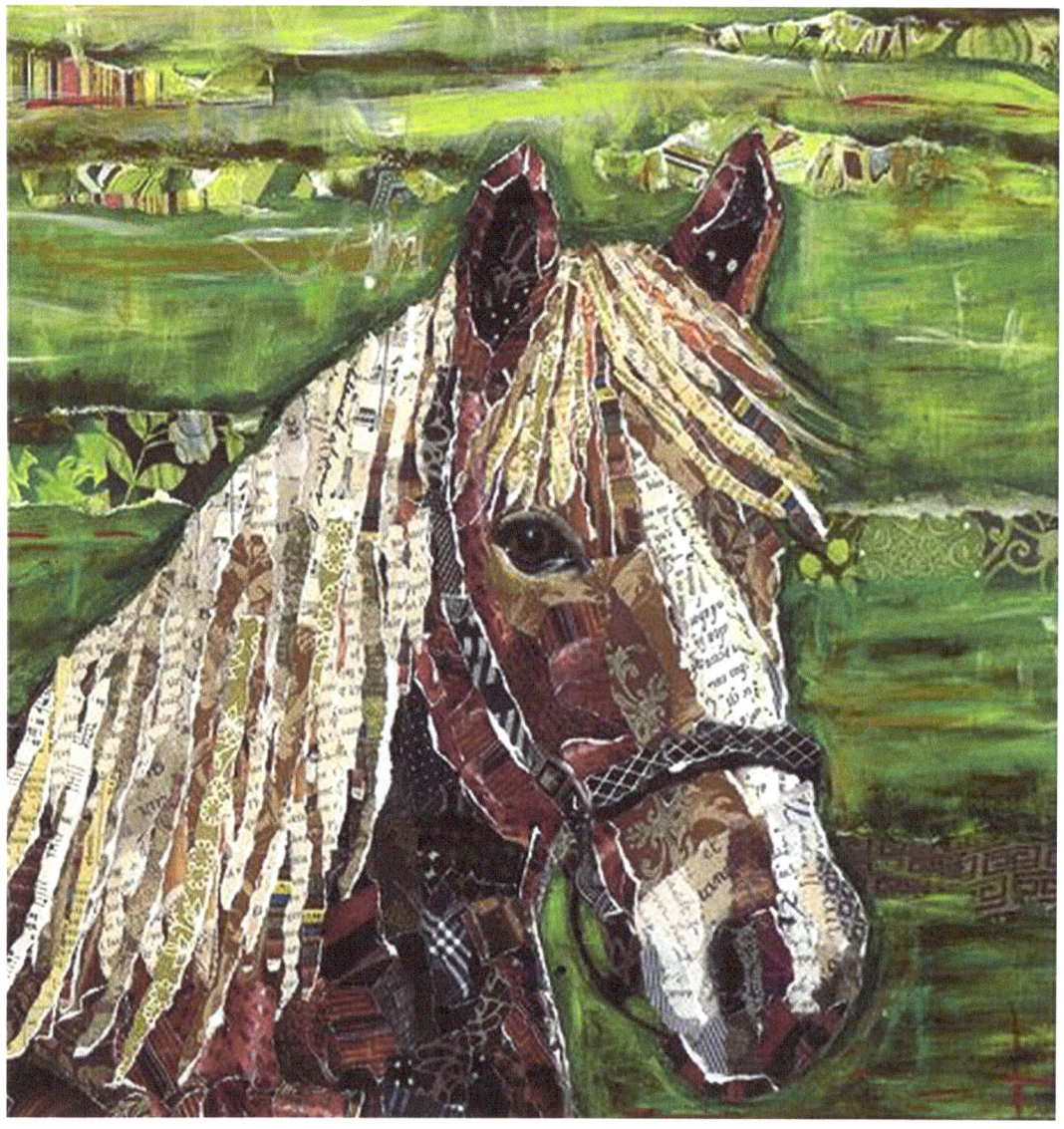

Farm Horse   *Susan Mcclellan*

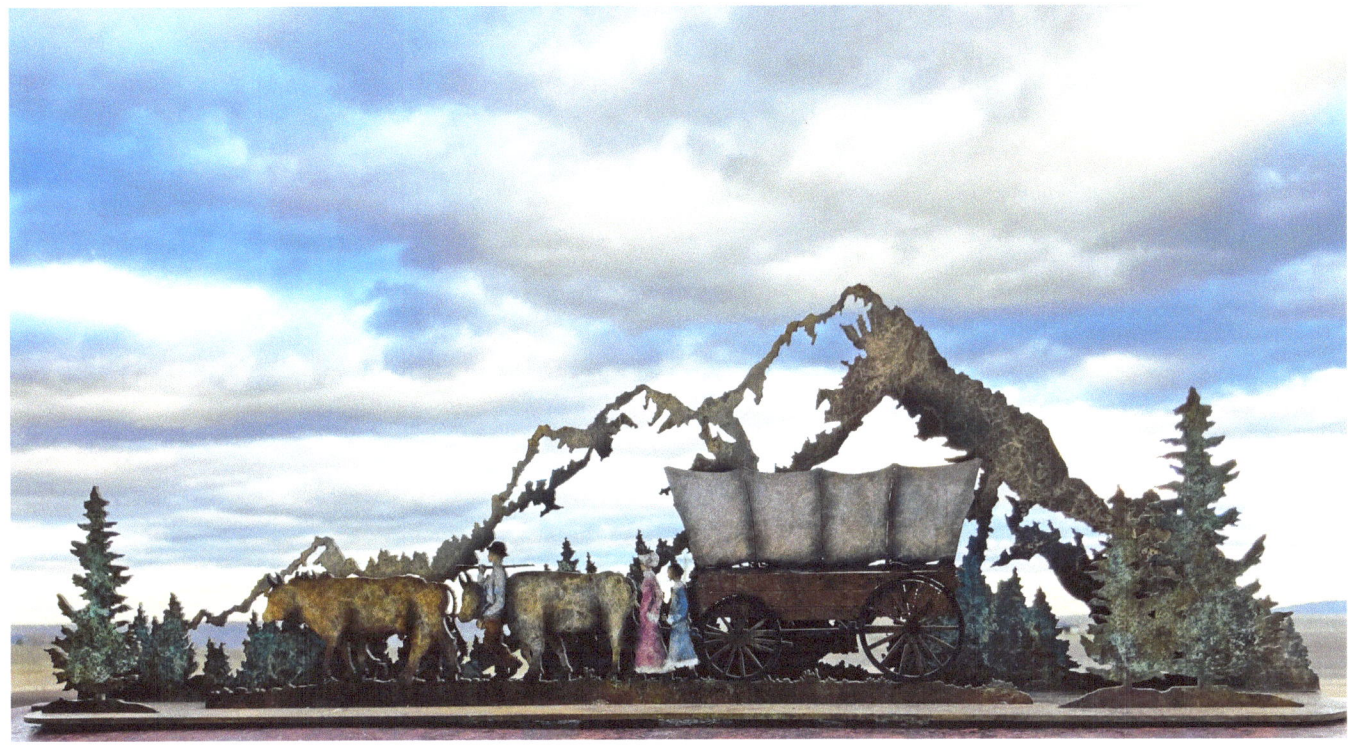

Covered Wagon Scene   *Erl McLaughlin*

Erl Mclaughlin was born and raised in in Steamboat Springs, CO. Graduated from Western State in Gunnison, CO with a Bachelor's of art in business and economics. He moved to Oregon and started teaching himself how to farm. He thought, "Maybe I've done this long enough," so he decided to start renting the ground and no longer have livestock, which freed him up to take care of his mom for 7 years. Enterprise reminds him of home in Colorado with the mountains. In 1983 Erl started collecting old tractors which expanded into an entire museum called Sunrise Iron. "My family has an art gene, my mom made quilts for veterans and babies in the county and my sister and brother in-law own Aspen Grove Gallery. Winters are long so I started making mantel pieces, coffee tables, wine tasting tables, chandeliers, and steampunk lamps among many other creations.

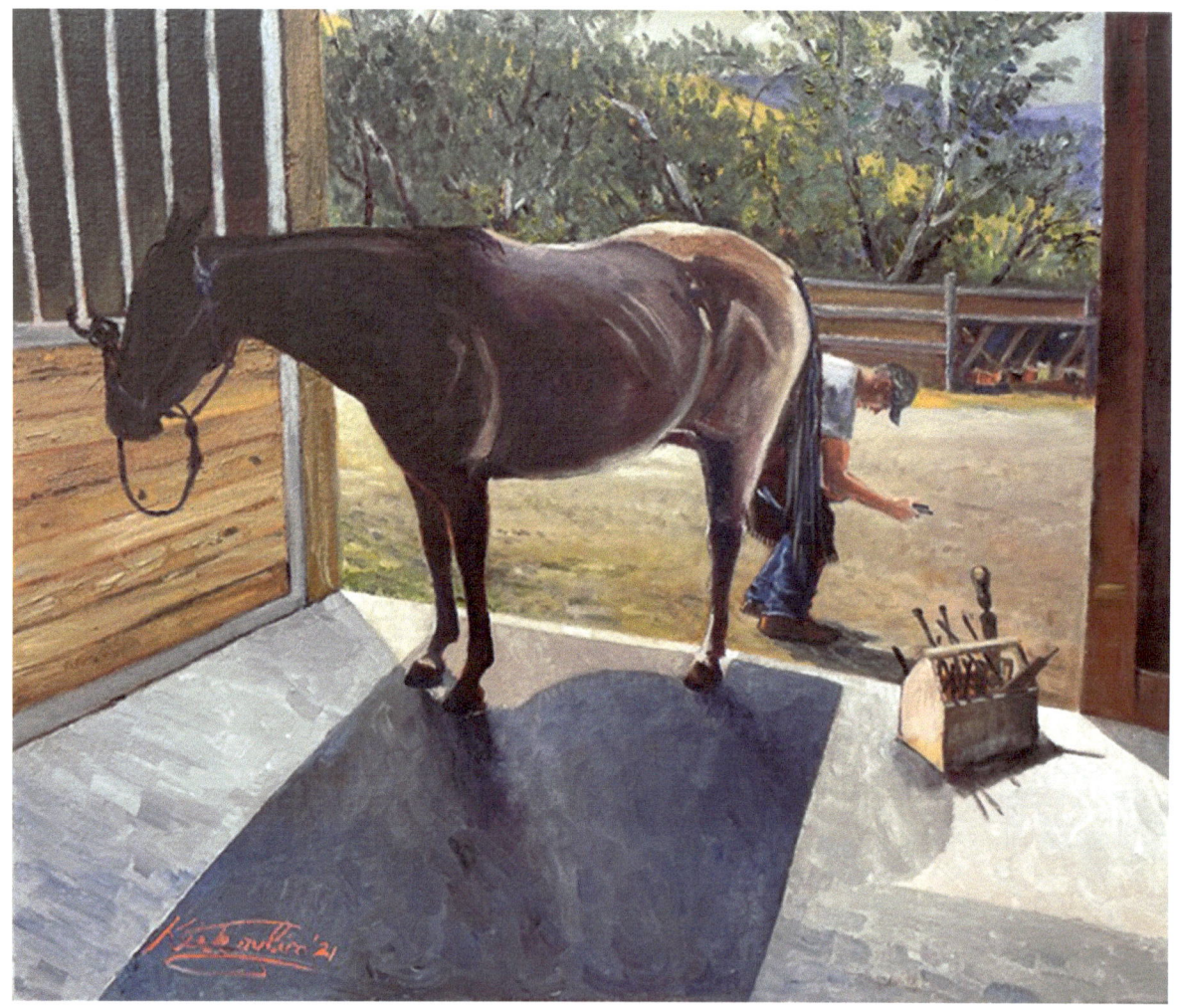

Waiting For The Dust To Seattle   *Kirk Skovlin*

I've lived in Wallowa County for 24 years and have roots here that go back to 1872. My ancestors moved here from Cove, bringing the first settler's livestock with them. The recent years living and working on the 6 Ranch has given me lots of inspiration to capture ranch life imagery and beautiful landscapes.

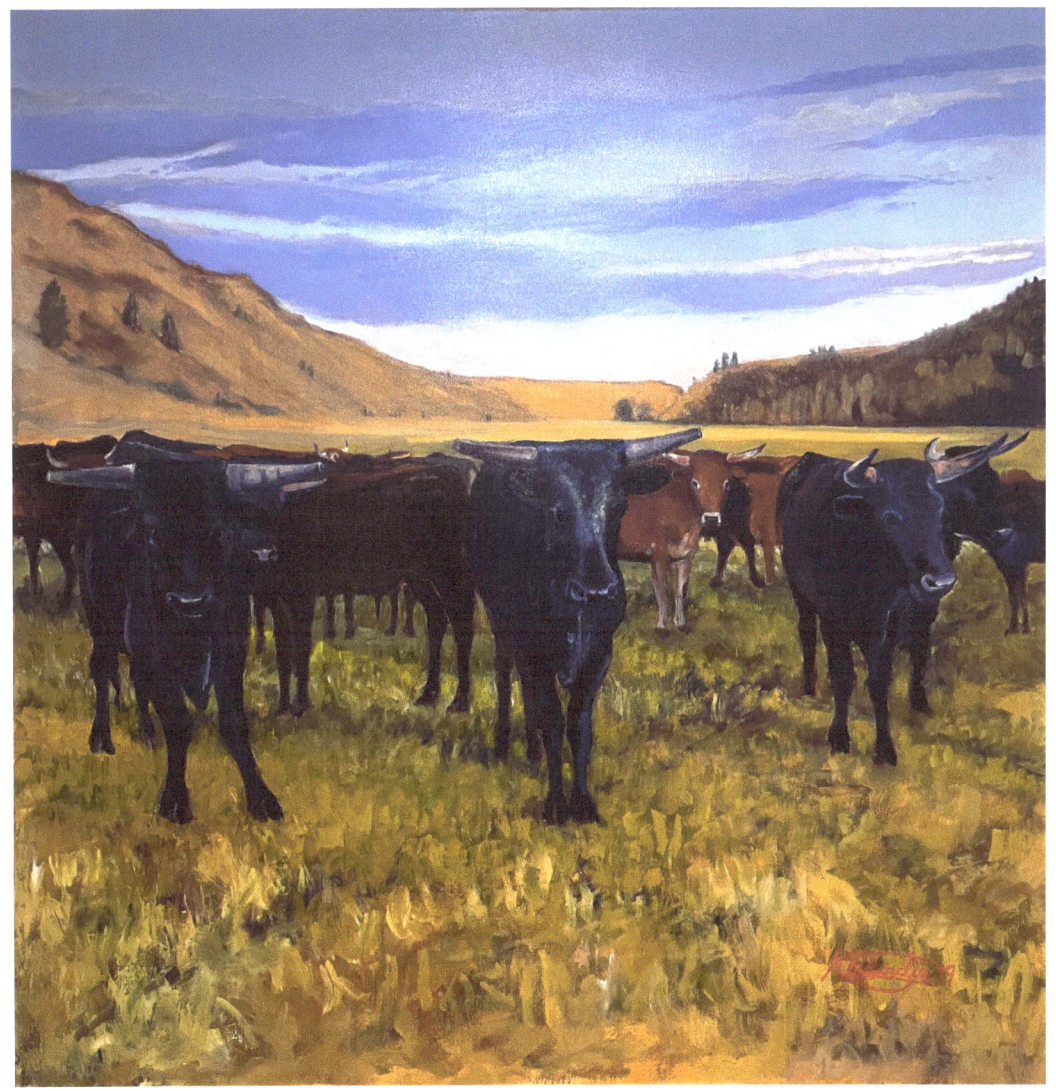

Grassfed Delegation   *Kirk Skovlin*

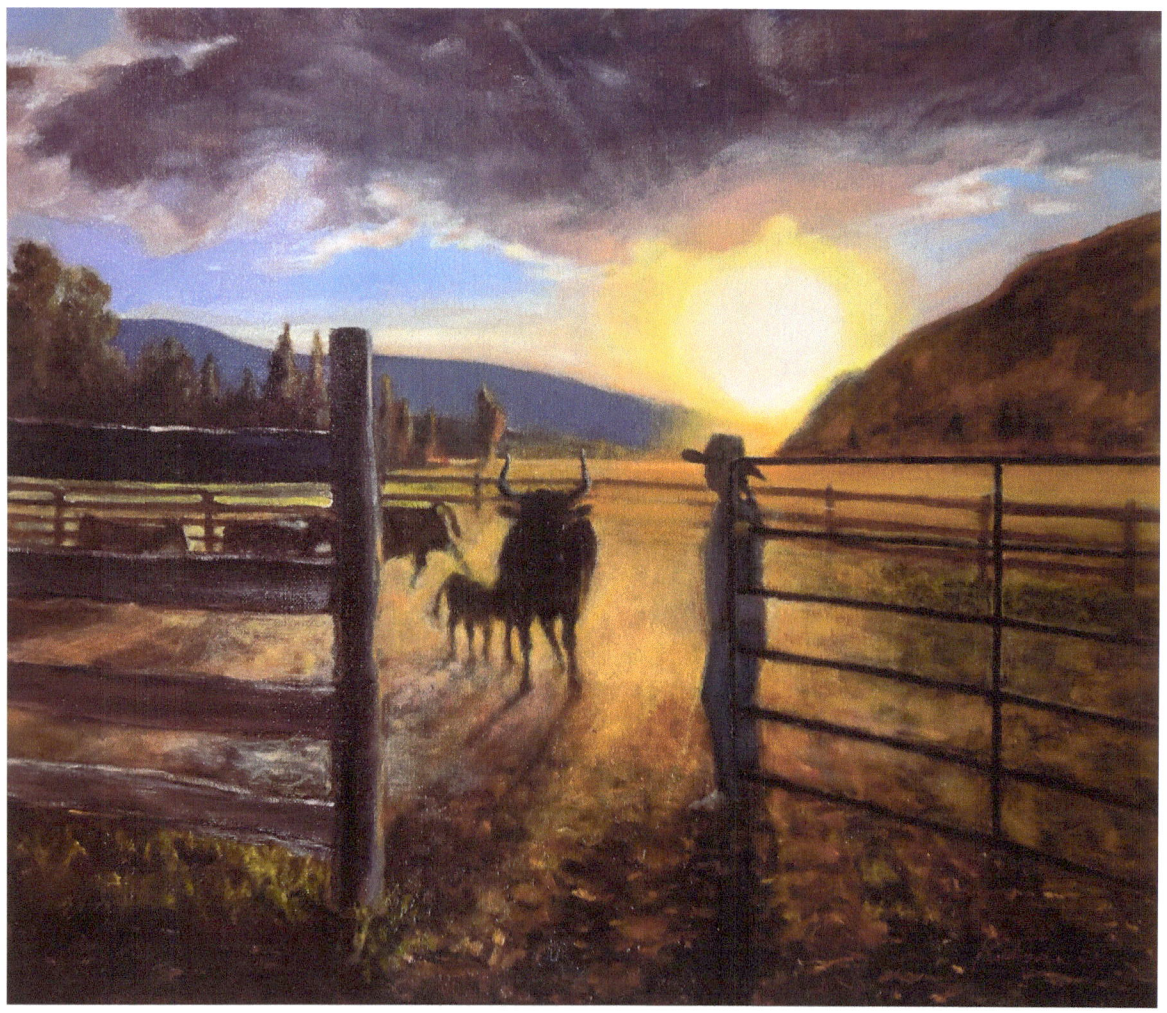

Reset   *Kirk Skovlin*

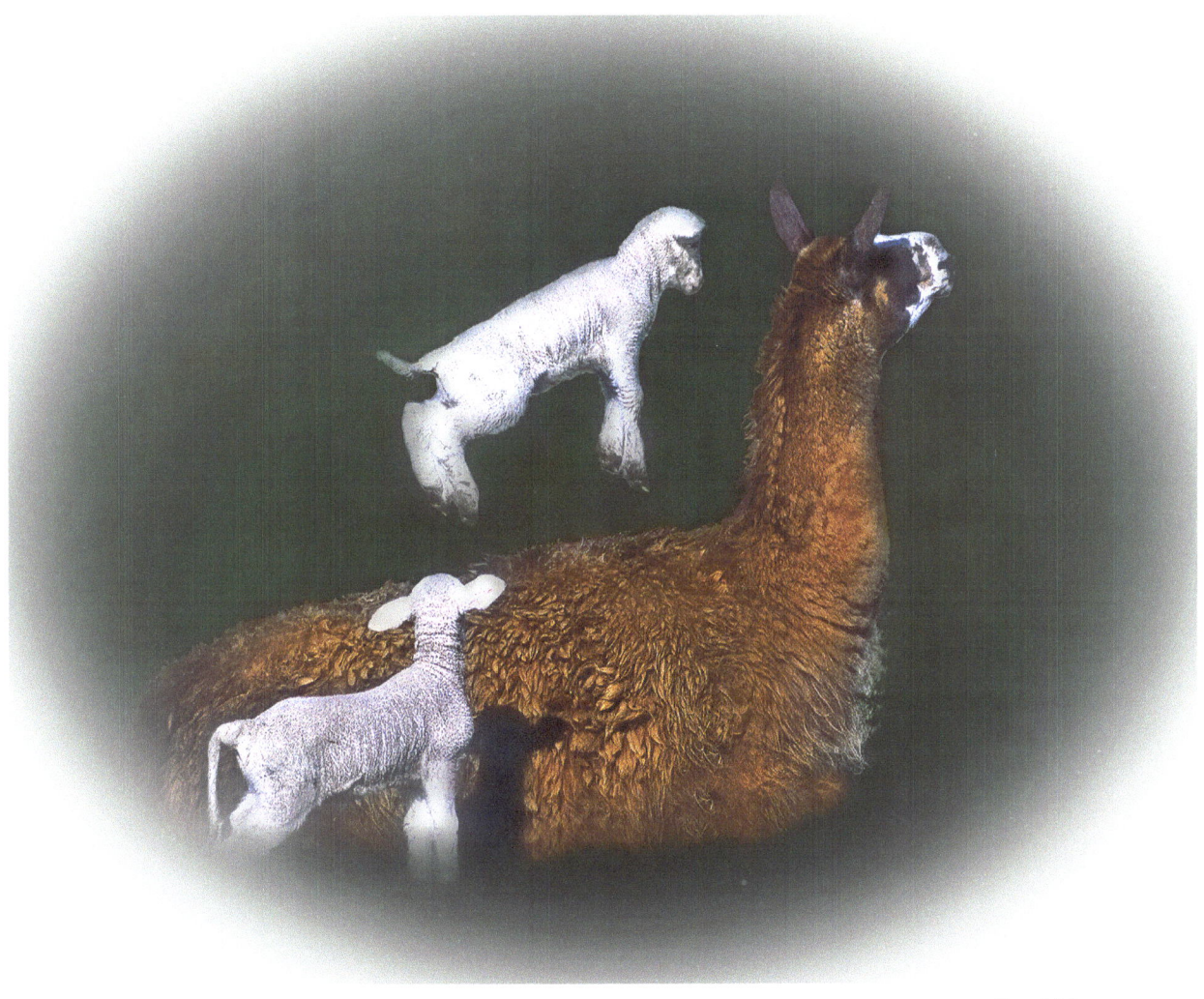

Guard Llama   *David Jensen*

Based in Enterprise, Oregon, David Jensen has been photographing eastern Oregon since the 1970s.

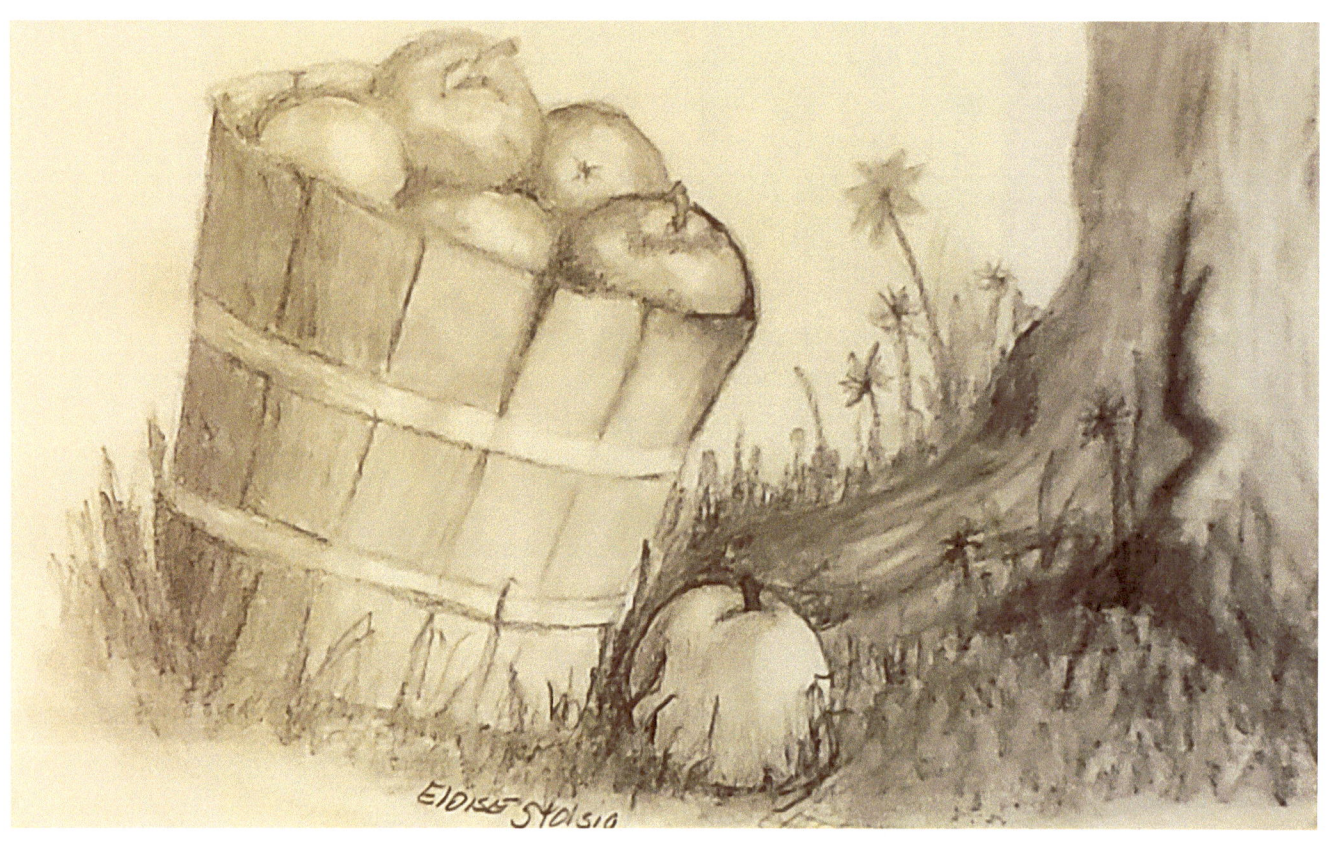

Apples   *Eloise Stolsig*

After living in Oregon for about 12 years I picked up a paint brush again
and have been having a ball ever since.

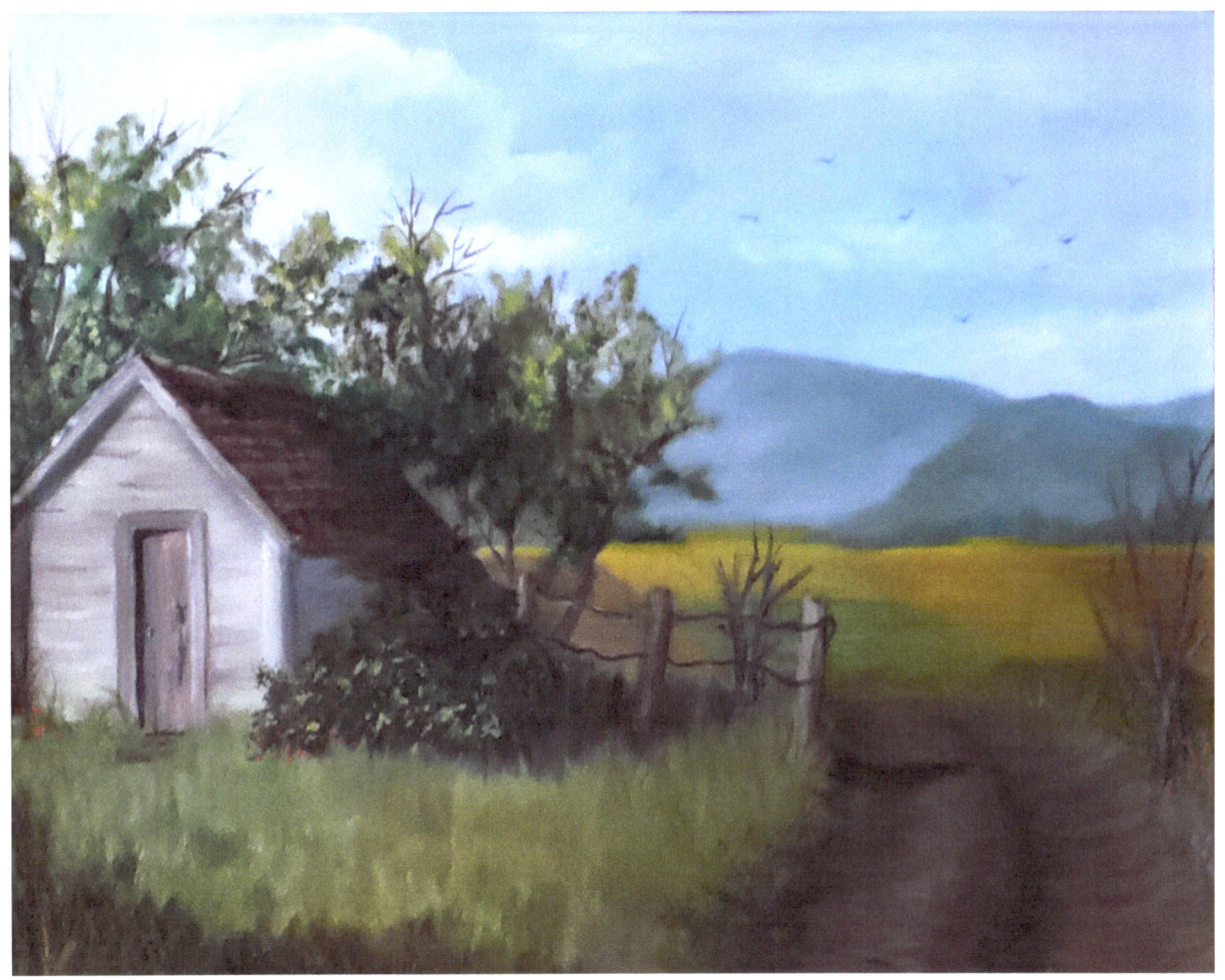

The Old Pumphouse   *Eloise Stolsig*

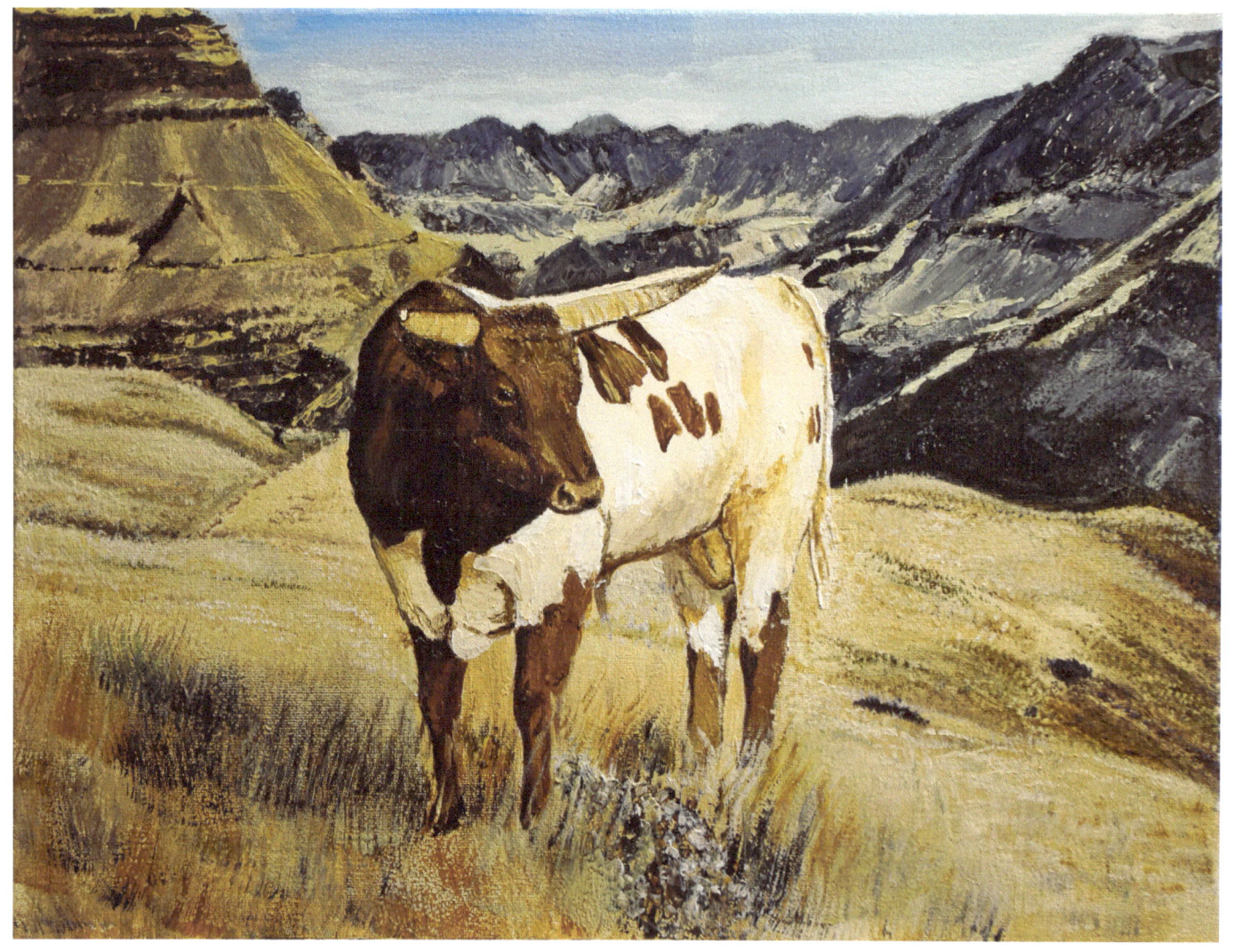

"Broken Horn" First Longhorn Bull Brought To Wallowa County   *Timothy Norman*

Drawing inspiration for my work from the beauty and grace of the natural environment, I strive to reflect
this in my paintings and bronze sculptures so the viewer can evoke a memory, emotion, or share
in a captured moment in time.